And such were some of you

C. Jack Orr

And Such Were Some of You

by
C. JACK ORR

For more than thirty-three years pastor of the Harmony Grove Community Church, Dover, Pennsylvania; presently engaged in evangelism and Bible teaching ministries. Currently chaplain of Willow Valley Manor Lifecare Community, Lancaster, Pa.

"And such were some of you; but ye are washed, but ye are sanctified, but ye are justified in the name of the Lord Jesus, and by the Spirit of our God" (1 Corinthians 6:11).

ISBN 0-914903-02-0

AUTHOR'S PREFACE

For twenty-seven years I was without Christ. In fact, I was without a witness as to my personal need of a Savior. In due time God set before me the way of salvation, and it was my job to receive Jesus Christ as my Savior and Lord. This life-transforming experience has led me into the Word of God wherein I learned that it is not only my duty to personally witness to others concerning His saving grace, but that it should be and is my soul's delight to testify to Jesus Christ.

Apart from the experience of salvation there is no greater joy for the Christian than that of introducing a soul to God's Son as "the Way, the Truth, and the Life" (John 14:6).

As I send this book on its spiritual journey, and as it makes its way into your hands, may it please God to lay upon you a burden for the lost, so that each day your prayer will be, "Lord, lead me as the prepared worker to the prepared heart today."

C. Jack Orr A 216
211 Willow Valley Square
Lancaster, PA 17602

DEDICATION

To Mildred E. Orr — my beloved wife,
my inspiration — with deep gratitude
to God for giving her to me.

CONTENTS

Chapter   **Page**

1   Christ Saves The Family   1
2   Watch God Work   5
3   A "Christian" Worker Was Lost   9
4   "Why Don't You Get Married?"   13
5   God Keeps His Word   17
6   The Woman Who Lived Three Days   21
7   A Heaven-Bound Salesman   25
8   A Jew Finds His Messiah   29
9   Saved and Married — In The Hospital!   33
10 Even Deacons Get Saved   37
11 One By One They Were Saved   41
12 Soul-Winning On A Jumbo 747   45
13 God Leads To The Prepared Heart   49
14 To The Altar Or The Lord — Which?   53
15 "V" Is For Victory   57
16 The Comfort Of The Word   61
17 No Accidents With God   65
18 The Man Who Read Books About Death   69
19 A Hopeless Man Makes A Decision   73
20 The Joy Of Our Salvation   77
21 God Saves Janitors Too!   81
22 A Tract Travels To India   85
23 "I Need To Be Saved"   89
24 Rock Band Leader Led To Christ   93
25 God Works In Strange Ways   96
26 Out Of Darkness Into The Light   99
27 Storms Can Be Blessings   103
28 The Man Who Wanted To Be An Ambassador   107
29 "What Is The Greatest Thing That Ever
        Happened To You?"   111
30 A Woman Set Free   117
31 Victory In Death   121
32 Faith Is The Victory   125
33 This Man Found New Life   129
34 He Thought He Had No Need   133
35 The Girl Made The Right Decision   137
36 Especially For You   141

FOREWORD

The Psalmist wrote,

> He that goeth forth and weepeth, bearing precious seed, shall doubtless come again with rejoicing, bringing his sheaves with him (Psalm 126:6).

In this great passage there is a **man**. God's method is to use men (and we use the word in the generic sense) to accomplish His work in the vineyard. And God has a **method** whereby the work shall be done. Soul-winning is an aggressive ministry in the sense that the soul-winner seeks out the person to whom he will witness. Soul-winning is not usually done in a rocking-chair; the Christian goes forth seeking the lost. And God prescribes the **manner** that should characterize the soul-winner. He goes forth weeping in the sense that he is burdened over the one to whom he witnesses, and most assuredly there are times when he will weep over that soul, whether in prayer or visibly before the lost one. In this hardened world of mankind, there are those who believe that no one cares; they are deeply moved to know that someone loves them enough to tearfully present the Word of God to them.

Then note that there is the **message**; it is described as seed, which obviously is the Word of God. There is but one message that can change the lives of men. The gospel alone can change hearts and homes; this is the Word that we bear to others. Then there is the **miracle,** the miracle of the new life. The worker has sown seed; he brings sheaves and presents them to the Lord of the Harvest. The seed has produced for God.

What a colossal ministry God has committed to us as believers in that we are called to spread the message of salvation. This being our responsibility, it is my joy to say that throughout my long ministry, I have never known a person to more accurately epitomize the message of the Psalmist than my beloved brother in Christ, and God's servant, C. Jack Orr. As a pastor and teacher of the Word of God he has excelled in one of the longest ministries in a pastorate with which I have been acquainted. This in itself speaks volumes for the ministry given him by God, but this ministry is enhanced by the fact that the larger percentage of those who constitute this great, working church have been won to Christ through his personal work with the gospel.

Jack Orr has been a joy to all who know him as a soul-winner. At times I have left his presence with a silent prayer that God would allow more of us to have the precious results from our work that the writer of this book has enjoyed. There is a price to be paid for the privilege of such a ministry for God. This involves much prayer for souls; it involves the consciousness that the responsibility for witness rests heavily upon each of us. It includes the conviction that souls are really lost, that time is running out for them, for us, for the Church, and that the time to witness is not tomorrow but today. Life hangs on one heartbeat for the sinner and for the servant of God. I know of no man personally who has taken to his heart these truths more seriously than the author of this book, and I consider him one most capable of producing such a work since his book is written not from a pedantic, theoretical viewpoint, but from the heart of one who has **done the work.**

I commend this book, **And Such Were Some of You**, as a work that will challenge and instruct. It will produce tears and tireless witnessing. It will be an inspiration to teacher and student alike, to pastor and people — here is a work from a man whose manner and message have, under God, produced miraculous results in terms of changed lives.

Gerald L. Stover
Lansdale, Pa.

INTRODUCTION

"You ought to write a book, Jack." The speaker was Jim Duffecy, International Director of Open Air Campaigners. I had been sharing with Jim some tremendous experiences of conversion and how the Lord was blessing my efforts in personal evangelism.

"Jack, why don't you write a book? I believe it would be a real encouragement to believers and reach many lost souls for our Lord."

I could not rid myself of Jim's challenge, but as a busy pastor I could not get time to work on it. About five years passed. During those years, time and again I would think of the book. Finally, the Lord laid such a burden upon my heart that I had to take action.

While talking with a Christian writer about plans for my book, she suggested the title: **And Such Were Some of You.**

Know ye not that the unrighteous shall not inherit the kingdom of God? Be not deceived: neither fornicators, nor idolators, nor adulterers, nor effeminate, nor abusers of themselves with mankind, Nor thieves, nor covetous, nor drunkards, nor revilers, nor extortioners, shall inherit the kingdom of God. And such were some of you: but ye are washed, but ye are sanctified, but ye are justified in the name of the Lord Jesus, and by the Spirit of our God (1 Cor. 6:9-11).

Verse 11 made a real impression upon my heart:

And such were some of you: but ye are washed, but ye are sanctified, but ye are justified in the name of the

Lord Jesus, and by the Spirit of our God.

As I read verses 9 and 10, I thought how they described the past. But the wonderful "buts" in verse 11 — "but ye are washed, but ye are sanctified, but ye are justified" — bring us to the present and to the future. You **were**, but you **are**.

You were, but you are washed from your sins, you are set apart by God, you are justified just as if you had never sinned. How can this be? Only in the name of our Lord Jesus . . . the only name that can make it possible.

Neither is there salvation in any other: for there is none other name under heaven given among men, whereby we must be saved (Acts 4:12).

But even then, how could it be done? The text from which the title of this book is drawn, **And Such Were Some of You**, gives the answer: "by the Spirit of our God."

I thought of my very own past. I was not a "down and outer." I was an "up and outer." According to the Word of God (Ephesians 2:12) I was an "outer" because I was without Christ, and without hope, and I was without God in this world.

Then I personally thanked God for the "buts."

But I am washed from my sins in the blood of Jesus Christ. I thanked God for the day that the Holy Spirit convicted me that I was a sinner and that God was holy. I might have measured myself by the standard of other people, but God said I must measure myself by His standard, "For all have sinned, and come short of the glory of God" (Romans 3:23). I knew that I was a sinner, and I knew that the wages of sin was death. But, thank God, the gift of God is eternal life through Jesus Christ, my Lord. I could by faith forsake all and trust Christ and be washed from my sins in His blood.

But I am sanctified, set apart by God positionally and, day by day, practically.

But I am justified. Therefore, being justified, I "have peace with God through our Lord Jesus Christ" (Romans 5:1).

Then I thought of those souls who have responded to the invitation of Christ as I have testified of Him. It is 1 Corinthians 6:9-11 in action.

No matter what your past has been, Jesus Christ died for your sins. He's alive. He will come into your life and you will be washed by His blood, set apart by God, and be justified in the name of the Lord Jesus and by the Spirit of our God.

I trust that you will be thrilled as you read of the power of the gospel of Jesus Christ to save souls and change lives. All the stories are true, only the names have been changed.

Chapter 1

CHRIST SAVES THE FAMILY

On January 7, 1942, kneeling at my bedside, I made the greatest decision of my life. I received the Lord Jesus Christ as my Lord and my Savior. Never will I forget the thrill and excitement as I read John 1:12:

But as many as received him, to them He gave the
power to become the sons of God.

I called to my wife: "Millie, I am born again!" I knew it on the authority of the Word of God. What joy was mine! Then on the very next night my wife made the same decision. We were indeed happy.

Then I became puzzled. Why had I not heard this good news before? That God loved me? That He gave His Son for me? That Christ died for my sins and rose again? That if I would receive the living Christ He would save me from Hell and transform my life? I determined that I would tell the world of Jesus.

Immediately the Lord put my father on my heart. Dad, like I, served on the board of our church, he read his Bible, he prayed, but I thought Dad was just like me and he did not really know of his need to make a personal decision to accept Christ as Lord and Savior. I asked my Dad if he would like to be saved. How surprised I was when he said "I am saved. I was saved when I was a small boy."

"But, Dad, you're the best dad a child could ever have, and I'm your only child, and I do appreciate all you have done for me. You have given me more than enough. But if you were saved, surely you knew that I was lost and going to Hell. Why didn't you tell me?"

1

I will never forget the look on my father's face as he said "I don't know. I just don't know."

I went to my mother and asked her to be saved, but she did not seem to understand. My mother was a very sick lady, and she feared hospitals. When a doctor recommended a hospital, I knew there would be a change of doctors. One day a doctor told her that she needed surgery and that it would be at a great risk. She might die. He wanted to send her to the hospital from his office, but she said: "I can't go today. I'll go tomorrow." That night she told me why she had made that decision. She wanted to talk to me. She wanted to be saved before she went to the hospital. What a thrilling thing it was to kneel with my mother and hear her in prayer ask the Lord Jesus Christ to come into her life and save her. What joy it was to read to her Romans 10:13: "For whosoever shall call upon the name of the Lord shall be saved." We, indeed, were rejoicing with those in the presence of the angels of God over a sinner who repented. Mother went to the hospital and to the operating room assured of the presence of the Lord and His promise: "I will never leave thee, nor forsake thee" (Hebrews 13:5).

The Lord was good and spared her life over great odds, the doctor said. Many years passed before Mother went to be with the Lord.

Dad had to go to a rest home. He could not walk or use his hands, but his mind was sharp. Ten months after Mother's homegoing I visited Dad in the rest home one day. He was in the television room with eleven other men. He was doing what I seldom saw him do: he was crying. It scared me. I said: "Dad, what's the matter?"

"I must see you right away."

I wanted to push his wheelchair to his room, but he said he didn't have time. And then he told me of his experience the previous night.

"At eight o'clock they dimmed the lights. Visiting hours were over. In bed, I began to reminisce. I thanked God for my parents. I thanked God that when I saw your mother as a beautiful young lady and asked the Lord to give her to me for my wife, He did, and she was as beautiful as she looked. I remembered asking God for a family, and you were born. And, son, I love you. I had asked God to give you a wonderful wife,

2

and Millie is the greatest. I had asked the Lord for a business, and He gave me that. I asked for a home, and He gave me that. Then I sang to myself — not out loud — but, suddenly, the Heavens became as brass. It was just a little after twelve o'clock. I had no assurance I was going to Heaven. From that time till 3:20 in the morning it was a hell on earth. I screamed, 'Oh, Lord, please don't separate me from you and my wife.' The nurses came running and said: 'Mr. Orr, you can't do this.' I told them I was sorry. I did not mean to be difficult. And then I prayed: 'My son is your servant. I will talk to him.' "

I was really shocked. I thought for sure my Dad was saved.

"You said you were saved."

"I thought I was."

"Tell me. Tell me exactly why you thought you were. Don't miss a detail."

He said when he was a little boy seven years old the churches were different than today. There were not fundamentalists and liberals. They all preached that one must be born again and that Christ died for our sins and rose again. When an invitation was given to come to the altar, he went. The altar was wet with his tears as he decided there to live for Christ.

"Dad, is that all you did?"

"What more could I do?"

"Mother and you got married in a church. Did going to the altar make you man and wife?"

"No, that's where it happened."

"What made you man and wife?"

"When I said to your mother before God: 'Mabel, I will leave my mother and father, and forsake all others, and take you to be my wife.' And she said, 'Curtis, I will leave my father and mother, and forsake all others, and take you to be my husband.' And then the preacher pronounced us to be husband and wife."

"Dad, did you ever doubt that you were married?"

"No, indeed."

"Dad, did you ever do with Jesus what you did with mother? Did you ever receive Him by faith? F-A-I-T-H, forsaking all, I take Him."

His eyes got so big. He said, "I never saw it that way. I believed about Him. I desired to live for Him, but I never

3

personally received Him." He bowed his head and cried: "Lord Jesus, I thank you for dying for my sins. I'm glad you're alive, and now I turn from all of my ways and I ask you to come into my life and be my Savior and be my Lord, and I thank you for doing it."

I'll never forget what followed. Tears streamed down his face as he said: "I'm saved, I'm saved. Thank God I'm saved!" And he really was. His life was changed completely. He told me that if anyone gave him five minutes he started telling them about Jesus. A friend passed and he asked: "Do you have five minutes?"

Two months later Dad was taken to the hospital. I was called. When I arrived a nurse said: "Pastor Orr, your father said 'Nurse, please let me go to be with Jesus.' **And he went.**"

Chapter 2

WATCH GOD WORK

My wife and I, with another couple, went to Florida for our vacation. While there we visited one of our missionary families. They were home on furlough and living on a missionary base. In their living room they had a sign: "Watch God Work." The sign looked like it was the work of one of their children. I thought to myself: "Why do they have that sign in their living room?" After an enjoyable day of fellowship, when we were leaving to go back to our motel, the husband embraced me, thanked me for our prayers and financial support, and said: "I want to give you a little gift as a token of our appreciation." It was a sign just like the one in their living room. I thanked him and took the sign home, and put it in a desk drawer in my study . . . certainly not on the wall in my living room.

About a month after our vacation, I was having my quiet time, and reading Philippians, chapter two, the Lord really spoke to my heart in verse 13:

For it is God which worketh in you both to will and to do of his good pleasure.

It is God which worketh in you! I thought of the sign. I took it out of the desk drawer. "Watch God Work." It was exactly what God was saying. "It is God which worketh in you both to will and to do of his good pleasure." He puts ideas in our mind and then He puts them into practice, and we have the thrill of watching God work through us. All of a sudden the sign became beautiful. I placed it on a door which I use each day. It added a new dimension to my ministry. What would God do today?

I went that day to visit with one of our members in the hospital. As I entered the hospital room, a nurse told me that Mr. Ziegler had been discharged. The gentleman in the next bed asked "You are a minister, aren't you?" Somewhat surprised, I said that I was.

"My name is Dale Wolford," the patient said. "I'm dying with cancer. Someone told me that in order to get to heaven you need to be born again."

"Yes," I replied. "Jesus said, 'Except a man be born again, he cannot see the kingdom of God' (John 3:3), and, 'Except a man be born of water and of the Spirit, he cannot enter into the kingdom of God' (John 3:5), and, 'Marvel not that I said unto thee, Ye must be born again' (John 3:7)."

"I don't know how to be born again. Can you help me?"

I showed him in John 3:16 how God so loved the world — and that he, Dale Wolford, was a part of that world so that God loved him so much that He gave His only begotten Son. I showed him that he, as is everyone else, is a sinner. Romans 3:23 states:

For all have sinned, and come short of the glory of God.

I showed him Romans 6:23: ". . . the wages of sin is death . . ." and that death means separation. If we die in our sins apart from Jesus Christ we must be separated from Christ throughout all eternity. But then I showed him the rest of that verse:

but the gift of God is eternal life through Jesus Christ our Lord.

You can't work for a gift, it would become a wage; you can't pay for a gift, it would become a purchase; a gift is something you can only receive. The cost of a gift is borne by the giver.

Dale saw with his physical eyes and with his spiritual eyes that it had cost God His Son and that Jesus died for his sins and paid his sin debt in full.

. . . how that Christ died for our sins according to the scriptures; And that he was buried, and that he rose again the third day according to the scriptures (1 Corinthians 15:3-4).

And now Dale personally could receive God's gift — the living Christ — as his Lord and Savior:

But as many as received him, to them gave he power to become the sons of God, even to them that believe on his name: Which were born, not of blood, nor of the will of the

6

flesh, nor of the will of men, but of God (John 1:12-13).

Dale asked the Lord Jesus to come into his life, take over his life, and become his Savior and Lord. We read together John 1:12 and 13. Dale not only knew how to be born again; **he was born again!**

Dale really fell in love with the Lord Jesus. He became a bold witness for his Lord. When he was discharged from the hospital, he was a very sick man. He spent a good part of the day reading his Bible and listening to Bible study tapes. He was weak in body, but so strong in spirit. He had a real desire to attend our church.

Physically, Dale grew worse and worse. Once more he was admitted to the hospital, and I was called there. One of the members of his family asked, "Pastor, how long will Dad have to suffer?" Just then I saw Dale take a last breath. "Your Dad just went to be with the Lord."

Dale's body went to our church for we had the memorial service there, but Dale was already with the Lord.

... absent from the body ... present with the Lord (2 Corinthians 5:8).

Through Dale's testimony, other members of his family came to know Jesus Christ as their Lord and Savior. I watched God work in the life of a man and his family.

This is the story of Dale Wolford! It is a true story. I had never seen him before. But God had him in the hospital that day instead of the member of my church that I had gone to see so that I could tell him about the love of God, the sacrificial death of Jesus Christ, His resurrection, and how Jesus desired to come into his life if Dale would receive Him.

And such were some of you. Maybe **you** have never been born again. You can be. You can receive Jesus Christ today as your Lord and Savior. Just bow your head, thank Him for dying for your sins, and ask Him to come into your life. **You, too, may watch God work.**

Chapter 3

A "CHRISTIAN" WORKER WAS LOST

Everybody needs a Savior. Everyone apart from Jesus Christ is lost and is headed for a Christless eternity. In Matthew 7:13-14 Jesus said:

Enter ye in at the strait gate: for wide is the gate, and broad is the way, that leadeth to destruction, and many there be which go in thereat: Because strait is the gate, and narrow is the way, which leadeth unto life, and few there be that find it.

Jesus is the spokesman, and He says that many are on the road to destruction and only a few are on the road of life. Another alarming thing, further along in the chapter in verses 21-23 Jesus said:

Not every one that saith unto me, Lord, Lord, shall enter into the kingdom of heaven; but he that doeth the will of my Father which is in heaven. Many will say to me in that day, Lord, Lord, have we not prophesied in thy name? and in thy name have cast out devils? and in thy name done many wonderful works? And then will I profess unto them, I never knew you: depart from me, ye that work iniquity.

Our story is about such a one. A Christian worker who was lost. **And such were some of you.**

In our church we had an excellent missionary. On this occasion we were having a series of great meetings. He mentioned that a dear brother who had worked with him in the field was an associate pastor of an evangelical Bible-believing church a few miles away, and asked if we might visit him some morning. We thought it was a great idea, so he called him on the phone to make arrangements. The pastor suggested that it might be better if they made the trip to us rather than our going to them so that we would not be pressured by time. He and his family came, and we had a wonderful time of fellowship round the dinner table.

After dinner I had an appointment to counsel with some parents. Telling my pastor friend how good it was to meet him and his family, I gave him one of my personal testimony tracts, "I Was Too Bad for Heaven but Too Good for Hell," and left them to visit with each other. As I went into my study with the parents, I really wondered why I had given the pastor one of my tracts.

That night we had a good time at the missionary conference. We had come home and were sitting at the table enjoying some refreshments when the phone rang. My wife took the call and said it was for me. To my surprise, it was my new-found pastor friend.

"Pastor Orr, I just read your tract and I have a problem."

"What's the problem, Pastor?"

"I'm not saved."

I asked him to wait till I could get to another phone in my study.

"Now, what you're saying is, you're not sure you are saved?"

"No, I am saying that I know I am not saved. I believe everything God says. I really thought that I was saved, but there was always that big question mark, and when I have led someone to the Lord it always bothered me."

I asked him if he really wanted to be saved, and there was an immediate "Yes."

"Do you believe that apart from Jesus Christ you are lost?"

"Yes."

"Do you believe that Jesus Christ died for your sins?"

"Yes."

"Do you believe that He arose again and is alive forever?"

"Yes."

"Is it the desire of your heart that He would come into your life and be your Savior and be your Lord, and take over your life and live His life through you?"

"Oh, yes; oh, yes!"

"Why don't you ask Him in right now?"

Broken before God, he asked the Lord Jesus Christ to come into his life and to rule and to reign. And in his prayer, he said "Thank you, Lord. Thank you, Lord. I'm free."

I asked him if he would be ashamed to tell anyone of his decision. "Oh, I want to tell everyone," he responded. I called his missionary friend and gave him the telephone to talk with the born-again pastor. I heard the missionary say: "Hello . . . yes . . . You what? Well, I'm rejoicing!" After hanging up the receiver, he commented on how foolish he felt and how surprised he was:

"I told you my pastor friend was a good brother. He was a great missionary. Why, his father was an evangelist. He graduated from one of the finest Christian liberal art colleges in the country. He graduated from one of the best Bible institutes in the country. He served under one of the great faith mission boards of our day. And he is now associate pastor of one of the great evangelical churches in our state."

But he, like others, was deceived by Satan. He believed all about and everything about Jesus, but there was never a time when he really received Jesus as his Savior and Lord.

John 5:39 describes part of his problem:

Search the scriptures; for in them ye think ye have eternal life: and they are they which testify of me.

And this he did. And he thought he was saved. But he never came to Christ and received Him as Savior and Lord. And the fortieth verse says "And ye will not come to me, that ye might have life."

The pastor was not a liberal. He did believe. But he never really received Jesus Christ as his Lord and Savior until that night on the phone. That night, however, with a broken and contrite heart he called upon Jesus to come into his life as his Lord and Savior. He passed from spiritual death unto spiritual life.

Verily, verily, I say unto you, He that heareth my word, and believeth on him that sent me, hath everlasting life, and shall not come into condemnation; but is passed from death unto life (John 5:24).

Could He who understands our thoughts afar off say to this

man now "I never knew you"?

How true, like Nicodemus, one can be religious and lost, sincere but lost. One can handle the Scriptures but refuse Jesus Christ His rightful place in his life. God loves the lost, whether they be dying thieves or a lost preacher. He stands willing to save either or both.

Chapter 4

"WHY DON'T YOU GET MARRIED?"

God puts great emphasis on the home. In Ephesians 5 God states the chain of command and how a home can be a happy one. As a matter of fact, a home should show a little bit of heaven on earth.

God has ordained that the husband should be the head of his home (Ephesians 5:22-24):

Wives, submit yourselves unto your own husbands, as unto the Lord. For the husband is the head of the wife, even as Christ is the head of the church: and he is the saviour of the body. Therefore as the church is subject unto Christ, so let the wives be to their own husbands in every thing.

We who are born again are to be subject to Christ. Wives, who are a type of the Church in fellowship with God, should be subject to their husbands. Husbands are a type of Christ. And the husband is supposed to love his wife even as Christ loved the Church and sacrificially gave himself for it.

Husbands, love your wives, even as as Christ also loved the church, and gave himself for it (Ephesians 5:25).

Then, the father is to bring up his child in the nurture and admonition of the Lord:

And, ye fathers, provoke not your children to wrath; but bring them up in the nurture and admonition of the Lord (Ephesians 6:4).

And then the children are to obey their parents:

Children, obey your parents in the Lord: for this is right. Honour thy father and mother; which is the first commandment with promise (Ephesians 6:1-2).

When we obey that chain of command, the home is indeed a home that glorifies the Lord Jesus Christ.

Dave and Beth were a fine couple. They had three dear children. They rented a house from one of my relatives. I got to know Beth and Dave pretty well because we would go fishing together once in a while. But then there came a time when we drifted away from one another, and I had not heard much about them for some time. One day someone asked if I had heard that Dave and Beth were separated. I just couldn't believe it. I figured she would be staying with her parents so I went home and called Beth.

"Beth, I understand that you and Dave are separated."

"Yes. Dave lost all love for us . . . for me and for the children."

"Beth, I'd like to help you. Could you come over to my study?" Beth said she couldn't drive, but that her father would bring her over. He did. He waited while Beth came into my study.

"Beth, what was the problem?"

"I don't know. All of a sudden he just said that he doesn't love us any more."

I drew a triangle. At the base of the triangle on one corner I wrote "Dave" and on the other corner I wrote "Beth." I explained to Beth that life is like a jigsaw puzzle and that sometimes we just have a hard time putting the pieces together. I said if I had Dave with us I would tell him that I was going to let him put some of its pieces out on the table and that I would let her do likewise. Then I would ask them why there was a gap. They did love each other once; they were a great family What happened? At the close of the discussion, I would put "Jesus" at the top of the triangle and then I would ask: "Beth if you would let Jesus come into your life and live His life through you; and, Dave, if you would let Christ come into your life and live His life through you, would there still be a gap? Beth said "Of course not." Then I showed her the truth of the Gospel — that Christ died for her sins and was buried, and that He arose again the third day according to the scriptures, and that Jesus really did want to come into her life.

Behold, I stand at the door, and knock: if any man hear my

voice, and open the door, I will come in to him, and will sup with him, and he with me (Revelation 3:20).

"You have seen pictures showing Jesus standing at a door knocking, haven't you?" She had.

"Beth, may I ask you an important question? How many times are you born?"

"Once."

I showed her a verse of Scripture and she read with me:
Jesus answered and said unto him, Verily, verily, I say unto thee, Except a man be born again, he cannot see the kingdom of God (John 3:3).

"Beth, if you were born again, how many times would you be born?"

"Twice."

And then I showed her John 1:12:
But as many as received him, to them gave he power to become the sons of God, even to them that believe on his name.

"The fact is," I continued, "Jesus died for your sins and rose again, and He does want to come into your life, and He does want to live His life through you. If you asked Christ to come in right now and take over your life, you would become a child of God. You would also become just the wife that Dave needs. Beth, you get to the top of the triangle and then maybe we can help Dave."

Beth made that decision in my study and received Christ as her Savior and, oh, she was happy. Her faith was almost stronger than mine.

"Shall I pack my suitcase? He is going to ask us to come back, isn't he?" I had to tell her that I just didn't know.

I called Dave that night about seven, before he went to work on the 11 o'clock shift. I told him I had heard about him and Beth, and that I had been able to help Beth that afternoon. I asked if I could talk with him. He was not interested.

"Dave, I am coming over to see you."

"Well, there is no need for you to waste your gas. If you insist on our talking, I'll come to see you." And he did.

As I drew the triangle and explained to him as I had earlier to Beth, Dave could not have been less concerned. He told me there was no unfaithfulness on anyone's part; it was just a lack of love. We stopped the discussion.

"Did you go fishing lately?" he asked.

"No, I was going to go tonight with my son." And I really did not mean to be dramatic.

"Why didn't you?"

"Because I wanted to talk with you."

"Well, I told you it wouldn't do any good."

But then he had tears in his eyes as he said, "Well, maybe it did a little good."

Next day I got a call from Dave and he asked if he and Beth could come to see me. He came in first and he told me there had been unfaithfulness and that he wanted to hear, as Beth had, how to be saved. And he, too, received Christ as his Savior.

It was such a joy to see those two embrace each other.

"It was well worthwhile," Beth said, "to have had such problems so we both could be born again."

And their little girl later on at home saw her Mom and Dad loving each other and didn't understand it. She said, "Mommy, Daddy, you love each other so much, why don't you get married?" Well, they were married, but she had not seen that love before Jesus Christ came into their lives.

And such were some of you . . .

Chapter 5

GOD KEEPS HIS WORD

Train up a child in the way he should go: and when he is old, he will not depart from it (Proverbs 22:6)

This is a promise of God. Many, many people, especially parents, are broken-hearted today because of rebellious, prodigal children.

And he said, A certain man had two sons: And the younger of them said to his father, Father, give me the portion of goods that falleth to me. And he divided unto them his living. And not many days after the younger son gathered all together, and took his journey into a far country, and there wasted his substance with riotous living. And when he had spent all, there arose a mighty famine in that land; and he began to be in want. And he went and joined himself to a citizen of that country; and he sent him into his fields to feed swine. And he would fain have filled his belly with the husks that the swine did eat; and no man gave unto him. And when he came to himself, he said, How many hired servants of my father's have bread enough and to spare, and I perish with hunger! I will arise and go to my father, and will say unto him, Father, I have sinned against heaven, and before thee, And am no more worthy to be called thy son: make me as one of thy hired servants. And he arose, and came to his father. But when he was yet a great way off, his father saw him, and had compassion, and ran, and fell on his neck, and kissed him. And the son said unto him, Father, I have sinned against heaven, and

17

in thy sight, and am no more worthy to be called thy son. But the father said to his servants, Bring forth the best robe, and put it on him; and put a ring on his hand, and shoes on his feet: And bring hither the fatted calf, and kill it; and let us eat, and be merry: For this my son was dead, and is alive again; he was lost, and is found. And they began to be merry (Luke 15:11-14).

One of the tremendous experiences I have had — and my life verse is Philippians 2:13: "For it is God which worketh in you both to will and to do of his good pleasure" — was on an occasion when I was doing visitation work in the hospital. On this particular day I was visiting one of our members and, in the course of our conversation, I looked at the man in the next bed in the semi-private room. I suppose he was in his sixties. He was a very, very sick man. He had cancer and he was suffering. He had been in and out of the hospital. As a matter of fact, when I left the room and checked the records, he wasn't supposed to be in that room at all, but somehow he was.

"Sir, how are you?"

"Not so good."

"What is your name?"

"Jonathan."

I immediately thought of the Jonathan in the Bible. "That's a good name, Jonathan. That's a Biblical name."

"You ought to know what my middle name is."

"What is your middle name?"

"David," he said.

"Jonathan David." I remembered David and his best friend Jonathan in the Bible, and I said his parents must have been Christians.

With tears streaming down his cheeks, he said: "They certainly were. I came up in a godly home."

I asked Jonathan how old he was when he received Christ. I never saw the man in my life. The tears continued to flow as he told me he had never received Christ.

"Jonathan, wouldn't you like to? Wouldn't you like to?" And I showed him the wonders of God's love. God so loved Jonathan David that He gave His only begotten Son; that Jonathan David was a sinner — just like everyone else — for all have sinned and come short of the glory of God; that Jonathan David had his

18

back turned on God and was going the wrong way toward a Christless eternity, for the wages of sin is death, separation from God. But God in His mercy allowed Jonathan David to be sick, even to be in this room, and God allowed my member to be sick and be in this room, and that God was seeking to save Jonathan David.

Then we retold the great truth, how Christ died for our sins according to the Scriptures, how He was buried, and arose again on the third day according to the Scriptures. And then I showed Jonathan his personal need of Jesus Christ. He knew it long, long ago because he had come from a Christian home. His father and mother believed Proverbs 22:6:

Train up a child in the way he should go: and when he is old, he will not depart from it.

"Jonathan, would you like to receive Jesus Christ right now?"

"I would."

I clasped my hand in his and I could feel from the warmth that his fever was high. With all sincerity and with tears on his cheeks, he said: "Lord Jesus, come into my life. Take over my life; be my Savior and be my Lord."

"Jonathan, did you really mean that?"

"I certainly did." And with joy on his countenance, he testified that Jesus was his Lord and he was born again.

I thought of what we'd read: "And when he came to himself, he said, How many hired servants of my father's have bread enough and to spare, and I perish with hunger! I will arise and go to my father." And he arose in repentance, received Jesus Christ, and was born again.

Train up a child in the way he should go . . . God says . . . and when he is old, he will not depart from it. God made a promise. God honored the faith of Jonathan David's parents. God encourages your faith if you have a rebellious child.

God specializes in saving rebels!

19

Chapter 6

THE WOMAN WHO LIVED THREE DAYS

It was in 1942 that I received notice that I was to report to Harrisburg for my physical examination for the military service. At that time, if you passed the physical you had ten days to get ready to leave. Then you received a month's training in the States, and then you were sent to Germany right into the thick of the battle.

I worked for Peoples' Service Stores then, and I was assistant manager of one of their chain stores. On the back page of the local newspaper were published the names of those who were to report to Harrisburg for physicals.

My last customer the night before I went for examination was a woman high in her seventies who operated a house of prostitution down the street. As I waited on her, she said:

"Doc, I read in the paper that you are going up for your physical examination tomorrow."

"That's right, Katie."

"That's too bad. That little boy of yours is really a dear. I watch your wife bring him in his walker to meet you. And that little fellow deserves to have his daddy at home. I'm going to pray that you won't pass."

I was shocked to hear Katie say that she would pray. I'm sure my facial expression showed my amazement, and I was a bit ashamed.

Next morning I was on the train with others who were to be examined. We arrived in Harrisburg and then were taken to the building where we would be examined. I did well with my examination until I got to the "heart" room. The doctor took my blood pressure. Then he took it the second time.

"Have you ever been sick?" he asked.

"No, sir, just a few colds and headaches . . . nothing serious." He took my pressure again. "Are you sure you've never been sick?"

"I'm sure."

"Lie down on that bed." Then he called three other doctors. They took my blood pressure. They checked my temperature. It was 102 degrees. The military doctor explained that I had hypertension and they would classify me as "4-F."

I really had mixed feelings. I loved America, but now I'd be home with my family. I called the manager of the store that night and gave him the news that I could open the store the following morning. My first customer was Katie. As she entered the store, she said: "You didn't pass, did you, Doc?"

"No, Katie, I didn't."

"I knew you wouldn't. I prayed over two hours for you last night."

Again, I was shocked. She, a woman who operated a house of prostitution, prayed for me for over two hours. Again I showed my amazement. This time very much.

"You're wondering how I pray, aren't you?"

"Yes, Katie."

"Doc, I know I'm no good. I don't ask God to do something for me. I asked Him to let that little boy have his daddy. And maybe sometime you can help me."

"I want to help you right now, Katie."

I took my New Testament out of my coat pocket and I read from John:

Jesus went unto the mount of Olives. And early in the morning he came again into the temple, and all the people came unto him; and he sat down, and taught them. And the scribes and Pharisees brought unto him a woman taken in adultery; and when they had set her in the midst, They said unto him, Master, this woman was taken in adultery, in the very act. Now Moses in the law commanded us, that such should be stoned: but what sayest thou? This they said, tempting him, that they might have to accuse him. But Jesus stooped down, and with his finger wrote on the ground, as though he heard them not. So when they continued asking him, he lifted up himself, and said unto them, He that is without sin among you, let him first cast a stone at her. And again he stooped down, and wrote on the ground. And they which heard it, being convicted by their own conscience, went out one by one, beginning at the eldest, even unto the last: and Jesus was left alone, and the woman standing in the midst. When Jesus had lifted up himself, and saw none but the woman, he said unto her, Woman, where are those thine accusers? hath no man condemned thee? She said, No man, Lord. And Jesus said unto her, Neither do I condemn thee: go, and sin no more (John 8:1-11).

I showed Katie in the Scriptures why all the woman's accusers disappeared: For all have sinned, and come short of the glory of God (Romans 3:23). And just like the one who was taken in adultery to be stoned to death, God said that for every sinner the wages of sin is death (Romans 6:23). Then I showed her in John 3:16 how God loved her and gave His only begotten Son. I showed her in Romans 5 how God commended His love toward her in that while she was a sinner Christ died for her, and that Christ is alive and wants to come into her life and transform her. I told her this was the miracle of the new birth. I showed her the invitation in John 1:12:

But as many as received him, to them gave he power to become the sons of God . . .

By this time, tears were streaming down Katie's face.

"I want to receive Him. I want to receive Him now." And she bowed her head and asked Christ to come into her life and be her Savior and her Lord. The display on the counter was wet with Katie's tears.

I asked her, "What did you just become?"

With great joy, she replied, "A child of God."

"How many times are you born?"

"Twice."

"If you had died last night, where would you have spent eternity?"

"In Hell."

"If you die today, where will your soul go?"

"Heaven!"

Then Katie told me that her family was of a different religion, and that on her 16th birthday her father went to an early Easter service and brought a man home and sold him Katie's body. That is how it all began.

Then Katie said: "Jesus Christ just put me out of business. I'm going to send the girls home." And she did.

Three days later Katie was found dead in her home. I remembered the question I asked her about where would her soul go if she died now. "Heaven" was her answer, **and Heaven it was in fact.**

Chapter 7

A HEAVEN-BOUND SALESMAN

For the Son of man is come to seek and to save that which was lost (Luke 19:10).

Jesus came first to seek. He seeks us, then He saves us. This indeed is the way it must be. Paul tells us, "There is none that understandeth, there is none that seeketh after God" (Romans 3:11). It is always God seeking us. We can go back to the Book of Beginnings — Genesis — to our first parents when they partook of the forbidden fruit. They knew then that they were naked and they made aprons of fig leaves to cover their nakedness. Then, when they heard the Lord coming in the cool of the day, they hid. And it was God who said, "Adam, where art thou?" God knew where Adam was, but He wanted Adam to know where he was. God seeks man.

How does God seek man? Through human instrumentality. This is one of the tremendous thrills of personal evangelism.

One morning I received a call from a lady who said, "Pastor Orr, one of your church members lives in an apartment in the same building I'm in, and she has been telling me that she knows for sure that she is going to Heaven. I really am disturbed. I need help. Can you come to visit me?" I told her I would be right down.

I found Linda with many, many questions. I helped her with some of her questions by showing her answers from the Bible. And then I asked her this all-important question:

"Linda, do you really know, or do you really want to know, that you are going to Heaven?"

25

"I don't know," she replied, "but I do want to know."

We sat at a table and I opened my Bible to John 3:16 and showed her that God so loved the world that He gave His only begotten Son and that whosoever believeth in Him should not perish but would have everlasting life. I told Linda that she and I are a part of the world that God so loved. We can put our names there. God so loved Linda that He gave His only begotten Son. Then I paged to the tenth chapter of the Gospel of John where Jesus said, "I am come that they might have life, and that they might have it more abundantly" (John 10:10). Life with purpose. Life with direction. Life that is filled with excitement. I asked Linda if she had ever enjoyed that kind of life. Then she related to me her past. It was full of discord and frustration.

I explained why her life was full of discord and frustration. As we looked at Romans 3:23 where we are told that all have sinned and come short of the glory of God, and then in the sixth chapter, verse 23, we are warned that the wages of sin is death.

"For instance, Linda, your husband is a salesman. He gets paid for selling. I get paid for preaching. And God said that we get paid for sinning. The wages of sin is death. Physical death means separation. My father and mother died ten months apart. I miss them very, very much. Spiritual death means separation from God. So, you see, our sins have separated us from God's plan, and if we die in our sins we would be separated from God eternally. But listen to the rest of this verse, Linda. The wages of sin is death, **but the gift of God is eternal life through Jesus Christ our Lord.**"

Then we paged to 1 Corinthians 15:3-4, ". . . how that Christ died for our sins according to the scriptures; And that he was buried, and that he rose again the third day according to the scriptures." This, of course, is the only way we can get to Heaven or else Jesus would never have gone to the cross. We looked at John 14:6 where Jesus, in answering a disciple's question about how we could know the way to Heaven, declared, "I am the way, the truth, and the life; no man cometh unto the Father, but by me."

But we must individually receive Jesus Christ. I showed her John 1:12: "But as many as received him, to them gave he power to become the sons of God," and I showed her John 3:3

26

where we are told that except a person is born again he cannot see the kingdom of God. In verse 5, Jesus went on to say that they cannot enter the kingdom of God; and, in verse 7, Jesus said, "Marvel not that I said unto thee, Ye must be born again."

"Linda, would you like to receive Christ? Do you want Him to come in and take over your life and live His life through you?" And she did. We knelt, and she asked the Lord Jesus Christ to come into her life, take over her life and plan it, and be her Savior and Lord. Oh, what joy was hers!

The following Sunday we were having a baptismal service in the evening and Linda was a visitor in our church. It was the first time she had ever viewed baptism by immersion. I called her on the phone the next day and asked how she liked the service. She said "Oh, Pastor Orr, it was really tremendous. I never heard anything like that. The testimonies . . . Could you come down next Saturday and talk to my husband Steve? And if he gets saved, could we both get baptized next Sunday night?"

I visited them the next Saturday. Steve was a traveling salesman who came home over the weekend. When Linda told him that he had an appointment with me so I could tell him how to get saved, he said, "Look, Linda, that's all right for you; but not for me. He's not going to see me."

Steve had to go to Hanover to get his weekly wage and when he got there his manager told him that he was discharged. He said he would take him home so he could drive back the company car. Steve's car was broken down, so Steve was at home.

Later, in the baptistry, after he had received Christ that Saturday afternoon, Steve gave this testimony:

"I was really frightened. I asked Linda if Pastor Orr was only going to talk to me, but she assured me he would talk with both of us. He did. He said, 'Hi, Linda,' and then he devoted the next twenty-five minutes to showing me how I could be saved. But I am so glad that he did, and that I received Christ as my Savior. **My wife and I are born again . . . Heaven-born and Heaven-bound.**

Chapter 8

A JEW FINDS HIS MESSIAH

In high school, I must admit that my great ambition centered on sports. I liked all sports. I played all sports. I especially remember two teachers I had in high school. I thought one of them was the best teacher I ever had; at least I used to think that. He would announce on a Monday morning that we would have an examination on Friday so that we would review Monday through Thursday. Now anyone who did not pass his tests really had to be a "dumbo." You crammed information in your head, you had it in your notebook, and — before I was saved — I even had it written on my cuff.

The other teacher — a Jew — was different. That fellow would come in on a Monday morning and hit you with a test that same day and we wouldn't be expecting it. Since I'm a man, since I'm saved, I have realized that the best teacher I had was the Jewish man. Who do you think I studied for?

It reminds me of the imminent return of the Lord. The reason the Lord doesn't tell us when He's coming is so we will always be ready. In my high school days, however, I was religious, but I wasn't a Christian. I didn't know what a Christian was. I wasn't saved until I was 27 years old.

One day after I was saved, after I had been preaching for some years, I received a telephone call from the lady friend of my Hebrew teacher.

"Pastor Orr, Benjamin's in the hospital. He's a very sick man, and he would like to see you."

I went to the hospital and I was rather surprised when I saw him. I was even more surprised when he asked a question.

"Jack, I've been reading about you, and I've been hearing about you, and you've been quite a successful man. What do you attribute your success to?"

"Ben, I'm sure it's not my intellect. If you remember back, you'll recall that you flunked me in high school. But it's not **what** I attribute my success to but **whom**."

"Whom do you attribute your success to?"

At that moment a student nurse came in. She said, "Pastor Orr, I will be going for my State board exams on Thursday. Would you pray for me?"Then she went out.

Ben said: "You're a busy man, aren't you? Praying for student nurses . . . praying for sinners like me. Whom do you attribute your success to?"

Then there was another interruption. They took Ben for some X-rays and then on to intensive care. He was burning up with fever.

I went up to intensive care to see Ben again.

"Ben, I'd like to share a verse of Scripture with you:

For I am not ashamed of the gospel of Christ: for it is the power of God unto salvation to every one that believeth; to the Jew first, and also to the Greek (Romans 1:16).

I explained to him how I had realized that I was a sinner. I had no purpose in life; I was just floundering around. And I knew that I would spend eternity in Hell. But then I saw in John 10:10 that Jesus came that I might have life and that I might have it more abundantly. And that He died on the cross for my sins, that He was buried, and He rose again. I said, "Ben, this Jesus is your Messiah."

I shared with Ben the Exodus 12 account where God, through Moses, said to take a lamb without spot and without blemish and kill it and put the blood at the top of the door and the side of the door, so that when the Death Angel passed by there would be security behind the blood.

And I showed him in First Peter that we are not redeemed with corruptible things such as silver and gold nor by vain traditions received from our fathers, but with the precious blood of Jesus Christ as a lamb without spot and without blemish (1 Peter 1:18-19).

Also, I showed him Isaiah 53:5-6:

But he was wounded for our transgressions, he was bruised for our iniquities: the chastisement of our peace was upon him; and with his stripes we are healed. All we like sheep have gone astray; we have turned every one to his own way; and the Lord hath laid on him the iniquity of us all.

"Ben, Jesus died and arose again for me, and He died and arose again for you. The only difference between us is that I have received Christ. I believed John 1:12, and I received Jesus Christ.

That man, burning up with a fever, said, "I believe Jesus is my Messiah." And he, too, asked Christ to come into his life.

The very next day he went to be with Jesus Christ. A Jew had not only received His Messiah; he was now WITH HIS MESSIAH.

Chapter 9

SAVED AND MARRIED — IN THE HOSPITAL!

Now a certain man was sick, named Lazarus, of Bethany, the town of Mary and her sister Martha. (It was that Mary which anointed the Lord with ointment, and wiped his feet with her hair, whose brother Lazarus was sick.) Therefore his sisters sent unto him, saying, Lord, behold, he whom thou lovest is sick (John 11:1-3).

Now that third verse sounds rather strange, doesn't it? ". . . Therefore his sisters sent unto Jesus, saying Lord, he whom thou lovest is sick." There seems to be a contradiction here. If Jesus loved him, how was he sick?

There are those who believe that all sickness is of sin. And we would agree that our first parents were created without sin, and it was sin that came into their lives and brought forth death. But not all sickness is because of sin.

Therefore his sisters sent unto him, saying, Lord, behold, he whom thou lovest is sick. When Jesus heard that, he said, This sickness is not unto death, but for the glory of God, that the Son of God might be glorified thereby (John 11:3-4).

It is this verse that brings to my mind the story of a young couple I was to counsel with one night.

We had just been seated when the telephone rang. It was one or our ladies who said, "Pastor, my cousin was to have been married on Friday in Maryland; but instead, her fiance became very, very ill with a bleeding ulcer. He is in the Memorial Hospital, and it looks like he might not make it. My cousin called and wondered if I could send my pastor to visit."

Needless to say, we got in the car and hurried to the hospital. When we got to the third floor and the intensive care unit, the young lady and her mother met me. They were much concerned, much distressed. I went into the intensive care unit where I saw this fine young man with tubes — several of them — giving him blood. He was a very sick man. We just had the opportunity to open the Word of God. I read from Matthew 14, beginning with verse 22, about the day that Jesus sent His disciples away in a boat while He went up in a mountain to pray. There was a great storm and the disciples were frightened. They saw Jesus then, coming walking on the water. No storm is too great for our Lord. He could walk on the same waves that would have destroyed them. And Jesus said a strange thing to them: "Be of good cheer; it is I; be not afraid."

Peter said, "Lord, if it be thou, bid me come unto thee on the water."

When Jesus said "come", Peter got out of that boat and he walked on the water to go to Jesus. But he made a mistake. The Lord had told him not to be afraid, but Peter got his eyes off the Lord and he looked at those waves and he was frightened. He cried, "Lord, save me." Now he was saved from his sins, but he meant from the storm. And immediately the Lord caught him, and they got into the boat.

I encouraged the sick young man and his concerned family to not look on the waters, on the storms of life, but to look to the Lord. I asked the young man if he knew he was saved; if he knew he was going to Heaven. He said: "Yes, I do." Then I looked at his girl friend and asked if she knew that she was going to Heaven. "I think so," she said.

"That's not good enough. If you are going to Heaven, you really know you are." And there in the hospital, I showed her John 3:16 and how God so loved the world, He so loved her, He so loved me, that He gave His only begotten Son. Why? Because she, I, and all of us are sinners. The Bible says in Romans 3:23 that all have sinned and come short of the glory of God. And Romans 6:23 says the wages of sin is death. We need to be saved, and 1 Corinthians 15:3-4 tells us that "Christ died for our sins according to the scriptures and that he was buried, and that he rose again the third day according to the scriptures." And He paid our sin debt. God can be a just God and still take us to Heaven. But we all need to be born again. Jesus said it three times over in the third chapter of John, and I showed them the invitation verse in John 1:12: ". . . as many as received him, to them gave he power to become the sons of God . . ."

"If you had gotten married last night, you both would have made your vows and each of you would have become the other's mate. Tonight Jesus wants to become yours, and He wants you to become His. Then you would become children of God."

There beside the bed of her boyfriend and husband-to-be, Rae asked Jesus Christ to come into her life and become her Savior and her Lord. And there was joy even in the time of sickness.

"Pastor, would you do one thing? If I can get those licenses transferred from Maryland to Pennsylvania, would you marry us?"

I agreed to marry them whenever he was able.

This verse became so true: "This sickness is not unto death, but for the glory of God, that the Son of God might be glorified thereby."

Oh, I trust that this story might help you, dear friend. Maybe you are going through a storm and you wonder how you can stand any more. There are many ways God can talk to you and you can come to know Christ as your Lord and Savior.

Oh yes, I married them in the hospital chapel. **They belong to each other — and to the Lord Jesus Christ!**

Chapter 10

EVEN DEACONS GET SAVED

There was a man, a very religious man who was a deacon in a local church. During an evangelistic crusade this man's sister-in-law had a real burden for him and his family. She invited them to the crusade and "in order to get her off our back, let's go," he finally said. So they went.

The evangelist was speaking that night on the Christian home. He exhorted on the chain of command from Ephesians:

Wives, submit yourselves unto your own husbands, as unto the Lord. For the husband is the head of the wife, even as Christ is the head of the church: and he is the saviour of the body. Therefore as the church is subject unto Christ, so let the wives be to their own husbands in every thing. Husbands, love your wives, even as Christ also loved the church, and gave himself for it (Ephesians 5:22-25).

Children, obey your parents in the Lord: for this is right (Ephesians 6:1).

And, ye fathers, provoke not your children to wrath; but bring them up in the nurture and admonition of the Lord (Ephesians 6:4).

This is the chain of command for the home.

Our friend listened to the message. As the evangelist gave the invitation, he said: "Every man should be the head of his home."

"My family knows I am the head," thought the visitor. "The neighbors know I'm the head of my home."

"But if you are not the spiritual head of your home,"

continued the evangelist, "then you are sending your children to Hell."

This was a blow. He knew that he certainly was not the spiritual head of his home.

The evangelist gave the invitation for people who wanted to be saved to raise their hands, but this man did not raise his. Then the evangelist invited everyone who wanted to be remembered in prayer because of problems they might have to raise their hands. This time, he raised his hand in response to the invitation. We prayed for him. He attended the rest of the crusade, but did not make any decision for Christ.

The crusade ended on a Sunday night. The next Wednesday night, because of the great victories in the crusade, we simply had a "praise night." We didn't preach that night. We invited people to get up and testify. Now the lady who asked the couple in question to church did not know that they were present that night sitting in a different location in the sanctuary. She praised the Lord for what the crusade had meant to her, and then she said, "My brother-in-law and sister were attending. I wish you would pray for them. They need to be saved." I remember that it caused my heart to take a couple of extra beats because I knew what she didn't. Her brother-in-law and sister were right there in the congregation.

At the close of the meeting I went to this couple.

"Dick, I know you heard your sister-in-law, and maybe you are a little bit embarrassed or frustrated, but I want you to know this: she is for you. I don't know where you go to church, and I don't want to know. But you raised your hand that you had a problem and requested prayer. I would like come and visit you."

We made an appointment for the next night. I went into their home the next night, and I was really scared. He was a big man who talks rather loud, and he said: "Does God always answer your prayers?"

"Well," I said, "He has answered a lot of them."

"He sure answered the prayer you made the other night."

"What was that, sir?"

38

"You prayed that if there was anyone here who was not saved that God would take away their sleep and their appetite until they had peace with God through Jesus Christ. And I haven't been able to sleep and I haven't been able to eat. I need to be saved."

We showed him God's simple plan of salvation. God loves the sinner — not the sin, but the sinner. God loves every individual. "For God so loved the world," John 3:16 says. Mark 16:15 teaches ". . . preach the gospel to every creature." We must personalize it, and I said: "God loves you, sir, so much that He gave His Son. Now the necessity of giving His Son is because you are a sinner and the wages of your sin is death. God is not only a God of love and a God of mercy, but He is a holy God and a just God. And God cannot condone sin and has warned that 'the soul that sinneth, it shall die.' But God sent His Son to take your place, to be your substitute, to be your sacrifice, to pay the penalty for your sins, and that was taken care of at the cross of Calvary. Jesus died, and was buried, and was raised again. He's the living Christ who wants to come into your life. And He wants to change your life. And He wants to live His life through you."

By that time, this big man was in tears. And not only he, but his wife also. And we knelt with them and they both received Jesus Christ as their Lord and Savior. And through a consistent witness for Christ, every one of their children came to know Jesus Christ as Lord and as Savior.

What a change in this man's life and in his vocabulary. He told me he used to pass Harmony Grove Community Church on Sunday nights and see all the cars in the parking lot and he'd think "Look at all those dumb people going to church." But now, if you come to the church, you can see this man and his family there. Jesus Christ makes the difference. Jesus **really** does make the difference.

Dick is now truly the spiritual head of his home. And, through his influence, his family also came to know Jesus Christ.

Chapter 11

ONE BY ONE THEY WERE SAVED

This family was separated because of sin . . . but God found them. I am reminded of a portion of Scripture in Acts 16. You'll remember that when Paul and Silas were placed in prison for preaching the gospel of Jesus Christ, the prison keeper was given the charge that his life would be taken if his prisoners escaped. The prisoners were beaten, their backs were bloodied, their feet were put into stocks, but they knew that they were where God wanted them to be. They probably did not understand it, but they were praying and they were singing praises unto God. No wonder the other prisoners noted what was going on. So many Christians complain, but not Paul and Silas.

Suddenly there was a great earthquake and the doors were jarred loose, and the prison keeper thought, of course, that Paul and Silas had escaped. He knew that meant he'd lose his life, so he pulled his sword and was going to commit suicide. "Do thyself no harm," Paul and Silas told him, "for we are all here."

Then the prison keeper called for a light, and sprang in, and came trembling, and fell down before Paul and Silas, And brought them out, and said, Sirs, what must I do to be saved? And they said, Believe on the Lord Jesus Christ, and thou shalt be saved, and thy house. And they spake unto him the word of the Lord, and to all that were in his house. And he took them the same hour of the night, and washed their stripes; and was baptized, he and all his, straightway (Acts 16:29-33).

The prison keeper and his whole family were saved!

The Bible says in John 3:8 that when we are born again it's like the wind: we don't know where it comes from or where it goes; so is everyone who is born of the Spirit.

But this family was separated. The wife was in deep sin. They had three beautiful children. They had moved into our area and wanted to keep their identity unknown. But school was starting and the mother worked and needed a place for her children to stay after school until she could get home from work. She didn't know anyone, so she rapped on doors in the neighborhood and came to one of our ladies. She told her story. She was all wrapped up in a cult and was about to be taken in as a member of the cult when she suddenly discovered that they relied on another book — in fact, two other books — instead of the Bible. She knew that wasn't right. She told the neighbor lady of her confusion and indecision, and the neighbor called me. I was just about to leave for an appointment, but she asked if I could help her. I said "Put her on the phone."

"Lady, I can give you twenty minutes. Can you come right down?" She came.

And her life, as she related it to me, was really mixed up. It was like a jigsaw puzzle with millions of pieces. But that day we showed her, even as Paul showed the prison keeper, the Word of the Lord and how God loved her, how Jesus died for her, how He is alive, and how He came that she might have life and have it more abundantly if she would just ask Him to come in and take over her entire life. There in my study in my home we knelt with her, and she asked Jesus Christ to come into her life, and be her Savior and Lord.

That was on a Wednesday morning. That night at our mid-week service, I went over to the church and there she was with her girls. One little girl was crying.

"What's the matter, honey?"

"My mother told me what happened to her this morning, and I want to be saved." I took her into my study in the church and she, too, was saved. Later the other daughters were saved.

The wife didn't know where her husband was. The husband didn't know where his wife and family were. But we started to pray. We put this family's needs on the prayer chain of our church.

One morning the husband woke up feeling different. He didn't seem to hate his wife or his family, and he felt like he'd like to see them again. Someone told him they'd heard that she was up in the Dover area. So he came to Dover and to the post office and asked for the name, but they could not give him information. He began riding all around Dover. He rode up Harmony Grove Road but, after some distance, he decided it was no use and he should give up. He was turning around in a lane that was marked "private" and the owner of that property meant it to be private so he came out in a hurry. "What are you doing here?"

"I'm looking for this family."

"Son, you are lucky. She lives right here."

It was just a little house. There was his wife and his children. They talked with each other. Now he really loved them and wanted them back. The wife told her husband of her experience, how she knocked on doors to find a place for her children after school, how she came to my study, and how Jesus Christ had saved her, and how for the first time in her life she had peace. Then he said "I want to see him."

I'll never forget the day that he came down. He was there when I came home, and my wife introduced us. He came into my study. God so convicted this man of his sin that he cried like a baby. He, too, realized that Jesus Christ was the only answer — that Jesus Christ was his only hope. He realized that Jesus Christ died for him and was buried and that He rose again and that He's alive — much alive — and that He wanted to make him just the man that he should be, just the husband that he should be, just the daddy that his children should have. We bowed with him and he asked Jesus Christ to come into his life. He went home and he and his wife were in love again. The children are saved. If you'd come to our church I could introduce you to these people.

At first there were some difficulties. The old life was still there. But they have grown in grace and in the knowledge of our Lord and Savior Jesus Christ. And now they are leading people to Jesus Christ. A young man has received Christ through their testimony.

The salvation of a whole household? Some would say "impossible," but **God answers prayer, and a home was saved! One by one they were brought to God.**

Chapter 12
SOUL-WINNING ON A JUMBO 747

Emory was sitting in a seat directly behind me on a jet 747 coming home from London, England, a trip arranged by God.

Our church people wanted to do something great for my wife and me and they thought one of the special things they could do would be to send us to the Holy Land so we could walk where Jesus walked and then go on to visit our missionaries in Europe. What a delightful trip it was. What an experience it was to go to Calvary and see the place where the Son of God laid down His life for sinners so that He might bring us to God, and then to walk into His empty tomb. During those twenty days I couldn't imagine anything greater than that experience, but one was to come.

When we got on the 747 in London for our return home, we were assigned seat numbers. During the flight a movie was shown. In fact, the plane was so large that there were three theaters. Knowing there would be some "jet lag" and that I needed to go to work the next day, I decided not to rent the earphones and watch the movie. I'd just recline and rest a bit. Since we were so near the screen, however, the flashing scenes kept me awake. Without the earphones the pictures didn't make much sense; but, like so many pictures, it had to do with two men and one woman. At the close of the picture I exchanged some comments about it with a young man sitting in back of me.

He asked where I had come from. I explained that we had been visiting in the Holy Land and also with our missionaries as a tremendous gift trip from our church. I told him how I had always wanted to go to the Holy Land but had never expected to because I wasn't able to afford the expense, and that this had been a tremendous and thrilling experience and a totally unexpected one.

"As a matter of fact," I added, "if anyone had told me I would become a preacher I couldn't have believed that either." And I began to share my testimony with him. I told him about the retired district superintendent of the denominational church I used to attend who was raising money for two colleges to help young men go into the ministry. He had said during his testimony that he knew when he died that he would go to Heaven.

At this point, Emory excitedly stood up and asked, "Did he tell you how he could know that?"

"No, no. I didn't ask him."

Emory sat down again.

"Do you know where I came from?" asked Emory. "I've been to Scotland. Do you know why? Two years ago there was a young man from a Bible Institute in Florida who told me the very same thing that man told you: That he was saved, he was born again, and that he was going to Heaven when he died. I didn't understand it all, but I have never been able to get away from that witness. And so I have been to Scotland to see a preacher who was my pastor when I was a small boy. I really wanted to find out the answer so I can know I am going to Heaven."

"Oh, I can tell you how you can know," I interrupted.

Just then the stewardess came to serve our dinner. But Emory said "Please, sir, tell me how."

"Emory," I said, "I'm not at all hungry. Let's talk."

I told Emory of my experience: How I had heard this minister give his testimony, how I became so angry I went home and argued with my wife that nobody could know for sure that they were going to Heaven, and how I had prayed that I would know if there was a way to know, and how God had led me to read in First John:

These things have I written unto you that believe on the name of the Son of God; that ye may know that ye have eternal life, and that ye may believe on the name of the Son of God (1 John 5:13).

46

And I showed him the things that were written that God had shown me:

For all have sinned, and come short of the glory of God (Romans 3:23).

I told him that he was a sinner and I was a sinner, and our sins deserved death — the wages of sin told about in Romans 6:23. Our sins deserve death, separation from God; but the verse doesn't end there. It continues: "but the gift of God is eternal life through Jesus Christ our Lord." And I showed him how God so loved him that He gave His only begotten Son; and how God solved the sin problem when Christ, according to 1 Peter 2:24, bore our sins in His own body on the tree so that He might bring him unto God; and how Christ arose again, according to 1 Corinthians 15:4; and how he could receive the gift of God — eternal life — in the person of Jesus Christ. John 1:12 assures us that "as many as received him, to them gave he power to become the sons of God."

Enter ye in at the strait gate: for wide is the gate, and broad is the way, that leadeth to destruction, and many there be which go in thereat. Because strait is the gate, and narrow is the way, which leadeth unto life, and few there be that find it (Matthew 7:13-14).

Jesus is the speaker and He is saying that many are going to destruction but only a few go in the narrow way and have eternal life. In Luke's Gospel we find the same teaching:

Strive to enter in at the strait gate: for many, I say unto you, will seek to enter in, and shall not be able (Luke 13:24).

I had had a problem with that word "strive" because the gospel had seemed so simple. And Emory was one who had to strive also. But there on that plane — I'll never forget it — Emory bowed his heart to the Lord. And he asked Jesus Christ to come into his life and to be his Savior and be his Lord.

Emory was a student, graduating that summer from law school. Now he is a Christian lawyer.

My friend, it wasn't easy for Emory. His struggle began with a young man's witness two years earlier. He had to strive to enter in at the strait gate. Perhaps he had not paid enough attention to the testimony he had heard, but God followed him. God knew his heart. God wanted to save him even more than

Emory wanted to be saved. And God arranged the Holy Land trip for my wife and me and our seats close to Emory on the trip home just so I could introduce him to Jesus Christ.

How exciting it is to serve the living Savior!

Chapter 13

GOD LEADS TO THE PREPARED HEART

The lady wanted some strawberries, she said, but, deep down in her heart, she really wanted to be saved.

Where we lived at the particular time, we had a strawberry patch. The season was ending, however, and when the lady called for some berries I had to tell her it was doubtful that we could find the eight boxes she asked for. She was persistent, though, and asked that we please check the next morning to see if there might be eight boxes.

When I awoke the next day I asked my son to go see if he could find eight boxes of berries for the lady. I was sure he couldn't, but to my surprise he came back with just eight boxes of berries. I don't know how we had missed them. But I called the lady to tell her, and I asked her to pick them up and put her money in the milk box since we planned to be away from home that day.

"Could you please bring them over to my house?" she asked. When I found out she was just about a mile away, I promised to deliver them.

When I took the berries to her, she told me that she would like very much to come to my church sometime, but that her husband would not come. She told me that her husband worked with one of our members and had been invited to attend our services.

"When you have been in the hospital so many times," she said, "and have been so very sick, you see things differently than someone does who is well."

I thought by this observation that she was a Christian. But when I asked her if she had been saved, she started crying: "No, that's why I wanted the strawberries. I wanted to talk to you."

That day I had the privilege of leading Helen to the Lord Jesus Christ. She received Him and, according to John 1:12, she became a child of God. She was born again, Heaven-born and Heaven-bound.

Now her husband Paul was a nice man, a real fine fellow. But he would look at people who said they were Christians and expect perfection. It just isn't there. You remember the apostle Paul said that he had not attained perfection but "I press toward the mark for the prize of the high calling of God in Christ Jesus" (Philippians 3:14). Certainly, we all make mistakes even though we are Christians. Paul couldn't understand that.

Later, Paul and Helen moved from Pennsylvania to Florida. We were always given a nice reception whenever we visited them. One year when we went to Florida, I felt in my soul that we should go to see Paul. I felt certain that this was the day that Paul was going to be saved. It was an experience something like the one Philip had which is recorded in Acts:

And the angel of the Lord spake unto Philip, saying, Arise, and go toward the south unto the way that goeth down from Jerusalem unto Gaza, which is desert. And he arose and went: and, behold, a man of Ethiopia, an eunuch of great authority under Candace queen of the Ethiopians, who had the charge of all her treasure, and had come to Jerusalem for to worship, Was returning, and sitting in his chariot read Esaias the prophet. Then the Spirit said unto Philip, Go near, and join thyself to this chariot. And Philip ran thither to him, and heard him read the prophet Esaias, and said, Understandest thou what thou readest? And he said, How can I, except some man should guide me? And he desired Philip that he would come up and sit with him. The place of the scripture which he read was this, He was led as a sheep to the slaughter; and like a lamb dumb before his shearer, so opened he not his mouth: In his humiliation his judgment was taken away: and who shall declare his generation? for his life is taken from the earth. And the eunuch answered Philip, and said, I pray thee, of whom speaketh the prophet this? of himself, or of some other man? Then Philip opened his mouth, and began at the same scripture, and preached unto him Jesus (Acts 8:26-35).

That text was taken from Isaiah 53, and Jesus was the Lamb, God's Lamb that was led to the slaughter and He opened not His mouth. And that day the Ethiopian eunuch was saved and followed the Lord in water baptism.

My experience was something like this. I didn't hear voices, but I just felt in my heart of hearts that I ought to go see Paul. There was another couple with us, but they agreed so we went to see Paul and Helen.

Helen greeted us in surprise. "Did you hear about Paul?"

"What about Paul?"

"He had a stroke and almost died." Then she told me something about his condition and that he was then asleep. Helen said they had a new young pastor and she asked that we pray that he would be able to make the gospel plain to Paul.

"Helen," I said, "I have to see Paul today. I believe in my heart of hearts that today is God's day of salvation for Paul."

She took me into the bedroom and awakened Paul.

As he raised his hand in greeting, I said, "Paul, I'm not going to do any little talk today. God has laid you on my heart, and I want you to rejoice for today is your day of salvation."

I took the Four Spiritual Laws, and showed Paul that God loved him and that God had a plan for his life. I told him that God loved him so much that He gave His only begotten Son (John 3:16) Who came that He, Paul, might have an abundant life (John 10:10). The reason that he was missing it was because he was a sinner — as we all are — and comes short of the glory of God. The wages of sin is death (Romans 6:23), and there is only one way to Heaven. Jesus told His disciples "I am the way . . . no man cometh unto the Father, but by me" (John 14:6). Christ died for our sins and was buried, and arose again the third day, according to the Scriptures (1 Corinthians 15:3-4). He could be born again and become a child of God if he would receive Jesus (John 1:12).

God was right about this being the day of salvation, and He had Paul ready just as He had the Ethiopian eunuch ready. There on that sick-bed Paul received Jesus Christ as his Lord and Savior, and he was wonderfully converted. He became a mighty testimony during the last few months of his life. He told everyone about Jesus Christ.

Now Paul is in Heaven. But what a thrilling story. How great it is to be used of God!

And such were some of you.

Chapter 14

TO THE ALTAR OR THE LORD — WHICH?

"Pastor Orr, I've never met you personally, but my son is a member of the High School Bible Club which you sponsor and he said to me, 'Mom, why don't you call Jack Orr? I'm sure he can help you.' Can you come visit me?" The lady's request was by way of a telephone call one evening. Looking at my calendar, it appeared that it might be a couple of weeks before I could go, so I asked her what her problem was.

"People tell me that I am saved, but I just am not sure of it."

"Tell me. Why would you think that you are saved?"

"Well, I went to the altar."

"What did you do at the altar?"

"Oh, I really don't know. But people tell me that I accepted Christ when I went and that I'm saved."

"It really doesn't matter what people tell you. You want to know. Let me ask you something: Do you believe you are a sinner?"

"Yes."

"Do you believe that God loves you and gave His Son?"

"Yes."

"Did you ever receive Jesus Christ as your Lord and Savior, sincerely believing that Christ died for your sins and was buried, and rose again the third day according to the Scriptures?"

"Well, I believe that but I'm not sure that I have ever received Him."

"You are a married lady, right? And you know that, don't you?"

"Yes."

"You've never doubted that you were married?"

"No."

"When and where were you married?"

She told me the date and the place. Then I asked her to tell me what happened there. And she said that she and her husband made their vows to each other and he became her husband and she became his wife.

"That's wonderful," I told her. "Now, have you ever done that with Jesus? I'm not talking about going to the altar, although it could have happened there, or in your home, or some other place. But have you ever had a time in your life when by faith . . . F-A-I-T-H . . . forsaking-all-I-take-Him?"

"No, sir, I haven't."

"Right now, on the telephone, would you like to take that step? Are you willing to turn from your sin, are you willing to forsake all and ask Jesus Christ to come into your life and be your Lord and Savior?" And over the telephone she did just that.

She rejoiced. She knew that she was born again. And she wrote the date in her Bible. What an unusual conversion, right over the telephone.

With this conversion and transformation of her life, she had a tremendous burden for her family and was grateful that her son was saved.

About this time in our city we were thinking about having a rescue mission, and a group of pastors and laymen went to Maryland to visit a rescue mission. Among the men who went on that visit was this lady's husband. I preached that night.

The following night my doorbell rang and there stood this husband and wife. And he said, "Pastor, last night as you preached, I saw my need of Jesus Christ. I didn't make the decision then, but I want to do it tonight. And he received the Lord as his Savior.

The rest of that family was saved. Her mother was saved. And what a tremendous blessing it was.

Seeing that family saved reminded me of the Scripture in Acts. You will remember that Paul and Silas were in prison and at midnight were praying and singing praises unto God:

And suddenly there was a great earthquake, so that the

54

foundations of the prison were shaken: and immediately all the doors were opened, and every one's bands were loosed. And the keeper of the prison awaking out of his sleep, and seeing the prison doors open, he drew out his sword, and would have killed himself, supposing that the prisoners had been fled. But Paul cried with a loud voice, saying, Do thyself no harm: for we are all here. Then he called for a light, and sprang in, and came trembling, and fell down before Paul and Silas, And brought them out, and said, Sirs, what must I do to be saved? And they said, Believe on the Lord Jesus Christ, and thou shalt be saved, and thy house. And they spake unto him the word of the Lord, and to all that were in his house (Acts 16:26-32).

Because God was seeking the lady who called me on the telephone, and I could speak the Word of the Lord to her and her family, I saw the whole family saved. An entire family believing and rejoicing just as the jailer and his family surely did. It is great to know that not only are they rejoicing now, but that they will spend eternity together.

Many people I have met along life's way have doubts about their salvation. Many are embarrassed to make these doubts known because they wonder what people will think. But it is so important to know, and the Bible says you can know:

These things have I written unto you that believe on the name of the Son of God: that ye may know that ye have eternal life, and that ye may believe on the name of the Son of God (1 John 5:13).

This lady wanted to know. If she had taken the advice of well-meaning people, perhaps even truly spiritual people, she might never have made her need known. She didn't need assurance: she needed salvation. She was trusting an altar. She was trusting a knowledge of Jesus Christ. But she was not trusting Jesus Christ to come into her heart and take over her life.

Have you ever made this decision? Do you know the time and the place where you forsook all and took Jesus? I trust that there has been such a time in your life. But if there has not been, today is your opportunity.

Today you can receive Jesus Christ. Jesus says that to as many as receive Him, to them he gives the power to become sons of God. Why don't you bow your head and just thank God for loving you, thank Jesus for dying for your sins, thank Him for being alive, and as the old hymnwriter said: "Just now your doubting give o'er, just now reject him no more, just now throw open the door, let Jesus come into your heart." If you do, John 1:12 will become a reality for you. **You will become a son of God. Think of that! A real . . . child of the living God!**

Chapter 15

"V" IS FOR VICTORY

But as it is written, Eye hath not seen, nor ear heard, neither have entered into the heart of man, the things which God hath preapred for them that love him (1 Corinthians 2:9).

I used to think this Scripture was referring to Heaven, but it isn't. It's talking about the experience we can have now. See how it continues:

But God hath revealed them unto us by his Spirit: for the Spirit searcheth all things, yea, the deep things of God. For what man knoweth the things of a man, save the spirit of man which is in him? even so the things of God knoweth no man, but the Spirit of God. Now we have received, not the spirit of the world, but the spirit which is of God: that we might know the things that are freely given to us of God. Which things also we speak, not in the words which man's wisdom teacheth, but which the Holy Ghost teacheth; comparing spiritual things with spiritual (1 Corinthians 2:10-13).

When we receive Jesus Christ as our Savior we are indwelt by the Holy Spirit. And this is what "eyes have not seen nor ears heard." But the unsaved man doesn't understand that. The following verse explains why this is so:

But the natural man receiveth not the things of the Spirit of God: for they are foolishness unto him: neither can he know them, because they are spiritually discerned (1 Corinthians 2:14).

You may have a doctor's degree and yet not be able to understand the Bible. You need to have a B.A. — "born again" — degree and then God will indwell you by His Holy Spirit and will reveal spiritual things to you.

Years and years ago a good friend of mine and I played basketball against each other. At that time neither of us was a Christian. We played a rough game: we played to win.

One day I received a phone call from a pastor friend of mine:

"Jack, I have our friend Harry here. He worked for me

today and I witnessed to him. I seem to have him up a tree and I can't get him down. He belongs to the same denominational church that you used to belong to. Wonder if you could run over and have dinner with us and give him your testimony."

On my way to join them I kept turning his name over in my mind and couldn't quite recall him. But when I went into the restaurant and saw him it came back to me who he was and when we had known each other. We recalled some of our basketball games and I suspected he thought I was one big hypocrite. He couldn't know the change that had come into my life when I received Jesus Christ.

I gave him my testimony: How I had heard a witness for Christ tell that he knew he was going to Heaven, how it made me angry and I had argued with my wife that night until she finally said: "Jack, you don't make any sense. There are only two places to go: Heaven or Hell."

I told him that really made an impression on me. I decided the next day I would go to my pastor and on my way also speak to the ministers of five other churches I would pass and ask them what the way to Heaven is. But I knew I would only be more confused if their answers differed. I told him how I went home instead and knelt in prayer and asked God to show me the way. I told him how God led me to 1 John 5:13:

These things have I written unto you that believe on the
name of the Son of God; that ye may know that ye have
eternal life, and that ye may believe on the name of the Son
of God.

I shared with Harry the verses that God the Holy Spirit directed to my attention that night. That I was a sinner and that "all have sinned, and come short of the glory of God" (Romans 3:23); and "the soul that sinneth, it shall die" (Ezekiel 18:4, 20). I knew that death meant separation and that I would be separated from God. But then I showed him the great news in John 3:16:

For God so loved the world, that he gave his only begotten
Son, that whosoever believeth in him should not perish, but
have everlasting life.

I told Harry that I put my name into that verse: "For God so loved Jack Orr" because I was a part of the world that He gave his Son for; and that Harry was a part of that world, too. God is a just God and He had said the soul that sinneth, it shall die. But Jesus, who knew no sin, because of His great love for us, died in our place as our substitute. He went to the cross of Calvary and laid down His life, bearing our sins in His own body on the tree, so that He might bring us to God. But He arose again the third day, according to the Scriptures, and today He is our living Savior. I told Harry how I asked Jesus to come into my life to be my Lord and be my Savior.

That day at that restaurant, Harry made that same decision. He asked Jesus to come into his life.

At that moment one of our members, who was then in nurses' training and was having dinner with some other students, came over to our table.

"Meet my friend Harry," I greeted her. Then I asked Harry to tell her exactly what had just happened.

"I was just born again!"

She rejoiced with us.

Harry went home and became an active witness for Christ. But within a few months he became a very sick man. It was diagnosed as cancer. He was hospitalized. In due time he couldn't talk. I would visit him in the hospital and Harry would put up two fingers in a "V" for victory. And he would strain to say: "Jack, I can't lose. I'm on the winning team. God can make me well, or God can take me to Heaven. I'm on the winning team." And he would flash that "V" for victory sign. Victory through Jesus.

You, and loved ones you may be concerned about, can make the same decision that Harry and I made. God says that "as many as received him, to them gave he power to become the sons of God." **There is nothing so wonderful as knowing that in Jesus Christ "V" stands for . . . Victory!**

Chapter 16

THE COMFORT OF THE WORD

The family was looking forward to a vacation. They needed a time of relaxation together and set out expectantly, but it ended in tragedy. Their little daughter drowned.

I noticed the news item in the paper about a little girl drowning while with her parents on vacation. Then the names of these people seemed to ring a bell and sound familiar. I checked the visitation cards of our church and found that they had indeed been our visitors. The paper indicated that the memorial service would be held by the chaplain of the hospital.

I visited Dick and Grace to express my sympathy. Their facial expressions were that of grief and as if they were taking a terrible, terrible beating.

I told them I would like to share with them what had happened to their little girl at the time of her death. I read from the twelfth chapter of Second Samuel:

And Nathan departed unto his house. And the Lord struck the child that Uriah's wife bare unto David, and it was very sick. David therefore besought God for the child; and David fasted, and went in, and lay all night upon the earth. And the elders of his house arose, and went to him, to raise him up from the earth: but he would not, neither did he eat bread with them. And it came to pass on the seventh day, that the child died. And the servants of David feared to tell him that the child was dead: for they said, Behold, while the child was yet alive, we spake unto him, and he would not hearken unto our voices: how will he then vex himself, if we tell him that the child is dead? But when David saw that his servants whispered, David perceived that the child was dead: therefore David said unto his servants, Is the child dead? And they said, He is dead. Then David arose from the earth, and washed, and anointed himself, and changed his apparel, and came into the house of the Lord, and worshipped: then he came to his own house; and when he required, they set bread before him, and he did eat. Then said his servants unto him, What thing is this that thou hast done? thou didst fast and weep for the child, while it was alive; but when the child was dead, thou didst rise and eat bread. And he said, While the child was yet alive, I fasted and wept: for I said, Who can tell whether God will be gracious to me, that the child may live? But now he is dead, wherefore should I fast? can I bring him back again? I shall go to him, but he shall not return to me (2 Samuel 12:15-23).

Now the little girl who drowned, like David's son, was of an age of unaccountability. And I showed those sad parents, Dick and Grace, how when their little child's heart beat for the last time that she immediately was absent from her body and was present with the Lord (2 Corinthians 5:6,8). The Apostle Paul said "to be with Christ . . . is far better" (Philippians 1:23). And I assured them that their little girl was even now in Heaven. Then I asked them if they knew that they would go to be with her. They sorrowfully replied, "No, Pastor, we don't." Then, of course, I unfolded to them the greatest story that mortal tongue could ever tell.

I referred them to John 3:16 which tells how God so loved the world — including Dick and Grace — that He gave His only begotten Son. Why was this necessary? Romans 3:23 tells us that all have sinned and come short of the glory of God. Unfortunately, that includes Dick and Grace too. All have sinned. In Romans 6:23 we are told that the wages of sin is death. God is a Holy God and we as sinners deserve separation from God. There is no way we could ever go to God apart from the love He has for us in the giving of His Son, Jesus, who died in our place so that we might be reconciled to God. ". . . Christ died for our sins according to the scriptures; And that he was buried, and that he rose again the third day according to the scriptures'' (1 Corinthians 15:3-4).

God is a loving God, a Holy God, and a merciful God. He is also a just God. He can be just and also a justifier of them that believe in Jesus. And I showed them how one can be born again into the family of God (John 1:12).

"Dick, Grace, is there any good reason why you would not receive Jesus Christ today?"

That Sunday afternoon I prayed with those parents, and both the father and the mother asked Jesus to come into their lives and be their Savior and Lord. And I showed them on the authority of God's word (John 1:12) that they were born into the family of God.

"How many times are you born?"

"Twice," they responded.

We read again John 3:16 about their everlasting life.

"How long is that?"

"Forever."

"Now, where will you go when you die?"

"Heaven."

Then I read again the verse in Second Samuel: ". . . I shall go to him, but he shall not return to me."

Could they bring back their daughter? Of course not. She could not come back to them, but they could go to her. And I saw the expressions on their faces change as God the Holy Spirit made real to them His eternal life through Jesus Christ our Lord.

They still sorrowed over the loss of their little girl, but not as those who had no hope. **They knew they were going to be with her again one day!**

Chapter 17

NO ACCIDENTS WITH GOD

There is none that understandeth, there is none that seeketh after God (Romans 3:11).

Many times people will testify that they "found" Jesus. The truth of the matter is, Jesus wasn't lost: the people were. And always it is the Savior who finds the sinner. This truth is expressed in Romans 3:11. And in Luke 19:10, we are told that "the Son of man is come to seek and to save that which was lost." And does He ever!

When we began our work at the church of which I was pastor, we had a very small congregation. Some of us were still talking in the parking lot after the service one morning when someone returned to tell us there had been a terrible accident down the road. One of our ladies was involved. An approaching car hit her head-on. I quickly went to the scene of the accident. Some people had already been taken to the hospital, and some to doctors, and one lady had been taken into the home of one of our members. I remember that she was lying on the couch in a lot of pain. I prayed and gave her verses of Scripture to comfort her.

I felt impressed the next day to visit this lady. When I rapped on her door, a daughter-in-law from next door responded and told me that both the man and his wife were in the hospital as a result of the accident. She asked if I was an insurance man. I told her that I was and I was with the greatest company in all the world. She asked what company that was. "The Eternal Assurance Company," but I hastened to explain that I was only kidding and was actually a minister. I asked her if she went to church anywhere. She didn't but said since the accident she'd been thinking about visiting a church nearby. And she told me how the accident had happened.

Her brother-in-law was home on furlough with his wife and baby, and the family had attended a church in York. On their return home, their little child was standing in the middle of the front seat and fell right on the steering wheel which, of course, turned and caused them to collide head-on with another car.

"If you had been in that accident and been killed, do you

65

know if you would have gone to Heaven?"

She said no.

"If I could show you in the Bible, would you like to know how?"

"Yes, I would. Come on in."

The first Scripture which I showed her was 1 John 5:13. Through "these things" — the Bible — I showed her how everyone needs a Savior. On that first Christmas, the angels said unto the shepherds who were watching their flocks by night: ". . . behold, I bring you good tidings of great joy, which shall be to all people. For unto you is born this day in the city of David a Saviour, which is Christ the Lord" (Luke 2:10-11). Now since all people need a savior, God's gift to man was Jesus Christ, His Son. Jesus came into the world to die for our sins because the wages of our sin is death. Jesus took our place there at Calvary. The only one who never sinned took our place and paid our sin debt so that He might bring us to God. And Jesus is alive, and we can receive Him as our Lord and Savior and be born again into the family of God.

In response to my invitation, we bowed, and she sincerely asked Christ to come into her life, and take over her life as Savior and Lord.

We looked at Romans 10:13: "For whosoever shall call upon the name of the Lord shall be saved."

"Did that 'whosoever' mean you?"

"It did."

"Did you mean it when you asked Jesus to come into your life?"

"I certainly did."

"What did He do?"

"He saved me!"

She asked if I could come back that night and visit with her husband. I had a meeting at a convalescent home until eight o'clock, but I told her I'd be happy to come after that.

When another member of our church and I pulled into their driveway that night, there was only a light in their bedroom and we hesitated ringing their doorbell. We prayed that if it was God's will, they would still be up. We rang and the husband answered the door and invited us in. He was expecting us, but he didn't look too friendly.

66

"Did your wife tell you what happened?" I asked.

"She just told me, and it's the craziest thing I ever heard."

I said that was the way it sounded to me, too, before I was saved.

"But, Dale, you do believe the Bible, don't you?"

He said he did. And I showed him how things were written in the Bible so that we might know that we have eternal life. We read the same Scriptures that I had earlier shown to his wife. I explained God's great plan of salvation, how God sent His Son to be our Savior, how Jesus took our place and died to pay our sin debt, how He was buried and arose and ascended into Heaven. I told him that this living Christ wanted to come into his life and make him a child of God.

That night that man received Christ. Since then, each of his children has received Christ as Savior and Lord.

That accident wasn't really an accident. **It was an occasion for God to seek and save sinners who were lost.**

And such were some of you.

Chapter 18

THE MAN WHO READ BOOKS ABOUT DEATH

A Christian nurse at the hospital one day asked me to visit a man in room 665. All his life this man has been afraid of death, she told me, and had read book after book about death. When someone was dying, he would even ask that he might go to their room and watch them die. He had asked the nurse what reaction she had when she saw people die. So this nurse thought it would be a good idea if I could go in and visit with him.

Tom was a sick man. I could see that.

"I understand you are interested in death," I said after greeting him and telling him who I was.

"Mister, I have read more books about death than most anyone, I believe, and I really am interested. As a pastor, you see people die. Tell me about it."

"Tom, I would like to talk with you about it, and I would especially like to show you what the Bible says about death."

I turned in my Bible to Genesis and told him of our first parents, Adam and Eve, who were sinless in the beginning, and how sin came into this world.

And the Lord God commanded the man, saying, Of every tree of the garden thou mayest freely eat: But of the tree of the knowledge of good and evil, thou shall not eat of it: for in the day that thou eatest thereof thou shalt surely die (Genesis 2: 16-17).   Now the serpent was more subtil than any beast of the field which the Lord God had made. And he said unto the woman, Yea, hath God said, Ye shall not eat of every tree of the garden? And the woman said

69

unto the serpent, We may eat of the fruit of the trees of the garden: But of the fruit of the tree which is in the midst of the garden, God hath said, Ye shall not eat of it, neither shall ye touch it, lest ye die. And the serpent said unto the woman, Ye shall not surely die: For God doth know that in the day ye eat thereof, then your eyes shall be opened, and ye shall be as gods, knowing good and evil. And when the woman saw that the tree was good for food, and that it was pleasant to the eyes, and a tree to be desired to make one wise, she took of the fruit thereof, and did eat, and gave also unto her husband with her; and he did eat (Genesis 3:1-6).

Adam and Eve sinned right then by disobeying God. Because of their sin, they died spiritually; and, later, they died physically.

Wherefore, as by one man sin entered into the world, and death by sin; and so death passed upon all men, for that all have sinned (Romans 5:12).

And as it is appointed unto men once to die, but after this the judgment (Hebrews 9:27).

Death is a reality, I told Tom. Death is something we all have to face. Now there are two sides to death: one side for the Christian, the other side for the unsaved. What happens when a Christian dies? God lets us know exactly what happens:

For we know that if our earthly house of this tabernacle were dissolved, we have a building of God, an house not made with hands, eternal in the heavens (2 Corinthians 5:1).

"Tom, we identify each other by our bodies; but the real you — your soul — lives within your body. And when this physical body dies, or dissolves, '. . . we have a building of God, an house not made with hands, eternal in the heavens.' "

We are confident, I say, and willing rather to be absent from the body and to be present with the Lord (2 Corinthians 5:8).

When a Christian dies, at the moment of that last heartbeat the soul is absent from the body and is present with the Lord. No matter whose funeral you attend, the one person who is not there is the one who died. The body is there and we view that but the soul of a Christian is already with the Lord.

Then I showed him verses such as Philippians 1:21: "For to me to live is Christ, and to die is gain." And Philippians 1:23, ". . . and to be with Christ; which is far better."

But what happens at death to one who is not a Christian? Well, it is a reverse process: the soul is absent from the body and is present in Hell, and the body is placed in the grave.

> . . . the rich man also died, and was buried; And in hell he lift up his eyes, being in torments, and seeth Abraham afar off, and Lazarus in his bosom. And he cried and said, Father Abraham, have mercy on me, and send Lazarus, and cool my tongue; for I am tormented in this flame (Luke 16: 22-24).

There are two resurrections: a resurrection of the just (the Christian) and a resurrection of the unjust (the unsaved). These resurrections occur 1,007 years apart. I told him of the resurrection of the Christian:

> But now is Christ risen from the dead, and become the firstfruits of them that slept. For since by man came death, by man came also the resurrection of the dead. For as in Adam all die, even so in Christ shall all be made alive. But every man in his own order: Christ the first-fruits; afterward they that are Christ's at his coming (1 Corinthians 15:20-23).

"Tom, not everyone will die. There are Christians who will not face physical death:

> 'Behold, I shew you a mystery: We shall not all sleep (die), but we shall all be changed. In a moment, in the twinkling of an eye, at the last trump: for the trumpet shall sound, and the dead shall be raised incorruptible, and we shall be changed. For this corruptible must put on incorruption, and this mortal must put on immortality. So when this corruptible shall have put on incorruption, and this mortal shall have put on immortality, then shall be brought to pass the saying that is written, Death is swallowed up in victory (1 Corinthians 15:51-54).'

"We all have corruptible bodies and they will be changed to incorruptible bodies and fashioned like the Lord's, whether we be caught up in the Rapture or raised from the grave. Death is an enemy. It separates us from loved ones, but it is swallowed up in victory because it becomes a vestibule that takes the child of God into the presence of the Lord where he will dwell forever.

After the coming of the Lord for His own, Jesus comes back to earth seven years later and reigns for a thousand years. Then the "white throne judgment" takes place, and the unsaved will be cast into the lake of fire to be tormented day and night forever and ever (Revelation 20).

"Tom, I'm not afraid of death. Do you know why?" Then I told him of my personal experience: how God showed me one day how much He loved me, that He gave His Son to die for my sins, and that Jesus died in my place as my substitute, and He arose again and ascended into Heaven and is alive. He came into my life and gave me life everlasting. And I showed him ". . . whosoever believeth in him should not perish, but have everlasting life" (John 3:16). And Tom, in his hospital bed, asked the Son of God to become his Savior.

Tom isn't afraid of death any more. He knows the date and the place where he received God's gift, Jesus Christ, and he knows that he now has everlasting life.

The man who read books about death, read "the Book" and found life . . . REAL LIFE.

Chapter 19

A HOPELESS MAN MAKES A DECISION

I met Bill when I first became the pastor of our church some thirty years ago. We had such a few people attending our church at first, and Bill's attendance was irregular. Then he didn't come at all.

Bill was a big man who worked with big equipment. He was what we know as a "man's man". I met Bill's mother, who was so crippled with arthritis that her hands looked more like pretzels than hands. But a godly woman she was. And even though I was not her pastor, and she went to another church, it was a real blessing to visit her. I would see her praising God in the midst of her pain. What a heritage Bill had! It reminded me of Paul's letter to Timothy:

When I call to remembrance the unfeigned faith that is in thee, which dwelt first in thy grandmother Lois, and thy mother Eunice; and I am persuaded that in thee also. Wherefore I put thee in remembrance that thou stir up the gift of God, which is in thee by the putting on of my hands (2 Timothy 1:5-6).

Before Timothy became a Christian, he had seen the example of a Christian in his mother and his grandmother. And I felt that Bill couldn't help but see Jesus Christ in his mother. Even though he stopped coming to church, and closed his ears to the gospel of Jesus Christ, he knew the truth.

Then we received word that Bill's mother had gone to be with the Lord. I went to his home to comfort him and his wife, a fine Christian who had also been praying for Bill. He had so

73

much going for him with a godly mother and her faith, and a godly wife and her prayers for Bill. That day when I visited Bill I read:

But I would not have you to be ignorant, brethren, concerning them which are asleep, that ye sorrow not, even as others which have no hope (1 Thessalonians 4:13).

"Bill," I comforted, "you are sad, of course, but you don't have to sorrow as those who have no hope, because you had a godly mother." I assured him that when he attended the viewing that night his mother's body would be there, but she would not be. His mother would be absent from the body and present with the Lord (2 Corinthians 5:8). And I read him God's promise of a reunion:

For if we believe that Jesus died and rose again, even so them also which sleep in Jesus will God bring with him. For this we say unto you by the word of the Lord, that we which are alive and remain unto the coming of the Lord shall not prevent (or precede) them which are asleep. For the Lord himself shall descend from heaven with a shout, with the voice of the archangel, and with the trump of God: and the dead in Christ shall rise first: Then we which are alive and remain shall be caught up together with them in the clouds, to meet the Lord in the air: and so shall we ever be with the Lord. Wherefore comfort one another with these words (I Thessalonians 4:14-18).

"Bill, your mother's body will be placed in the grave tomorrow. But it's going to be a great day when Jesus comes and your mother's body will be raised an incorruptible body and be reunited with her soul which is already present with the Lord. And we who have put our trust in the Lord, if we are still living then, will be caught up with our loved ones to meet the Lord in the air, and so shall we ever be with the Lord. So sorrow not as those who have no hope."

Then I asked Bill: "Have you ever received Jesus as your Lord and Savior?"

"No, I haven't."

"Would you like to do that?"

I'll never forget this giant of a man who must have weighed nearly 280 pounds, sitting in an easy chair, just sitting there looking at me.

"Bill," I repeated, "would you like to receive Jesus as your Lord and Savior?"

Still he sat there staring at me.

"Bill, will you just answer? You must do something with Jesus. Either you receive Him or you reject Him. And your mother prayed for you, your wife prays for you, I pray for you, other people are praying for you. Don't you want to accept Christ as your Savior today?"

He just sat there.

I told Bill I had to go home. It was a cold winter day so I put on my topcoat. As I went toward the door, I don't think I ever had such a burden for a man, such love for one, and I got down on my knees at his easy chair and put my arms around Bill and wept.

"Bill, please do accept Jesus Christ as your Lord and Savior."

"I will!" He said it in a loud voice. I'll never forget it. Bill welcomed Christ into his life as his Savior.

Bill's life was transformed by the power of the gospel of Jesus Christ. He went to church regularly. Then he became ill. He had cancer. He dwindled away from nearly 280 to just over 100 pounds. But in the hospital he was a witness to everybody about what Jesus Christ had done for him. One day we received the word that Bill had gone to be with his Lord. He was absent from the body and present with the Lord.

Bill was lost and he was difficult to win, but then he responded to God's love and said, "Yes, I will" receive Jesus.

I don't know when this wonderful event that we read about in First Thessalonians 4:13-18 will take place, but we do know that when the trumpet of God sounds, the dead in Christ shall rise first and those saved ones who are still alive will meet the Lord in the air and so shall we ever be with the Lord.

Our God specializes in giving hope to the hopeless!

Chapter 20

THE JOY OF OUR SALVATION

The second most thrilling thing in my life is to live for Jesus. The first most thrilling experience was, of course, the receiving of Jesus as my Lord and Savior. My life verse is:

For it is God which worketh in you both to will and to do of his good pleasure (Philippians 2:13).

And this is so exciting . . . I remember, for instance, the time that God put into my mind, and then into my feet my meeting of Ted and Marie.

I was visiting one hospital and then another about 3:30 one afternoon. A storm was coming up, and it was so dark I had to use my headlights. The parking lot of the second hospital was filled, I couldn't find a place to park, and the thought crossed my mind that I really should just go on home. I breathed a prayer that if God wanted me to visit in the hospital that day there would be a parking space. Just then a car backed out of a place, and I pulled in.

I was going through the waiting room, heading for the one patient I had come to see, when I met a man I hadn't seen for quite a while. He used to be my insurance man. Ted was the district manager of an insurance company.

"Jack, I want to see you." And Ted told me that they had been on their vacation when his wife became ill while visiting a big city in New England. He had to take her to the hospital, and surgery confirmed that she was full of cancer. The doctors there could do nothing more for her and suggested that he bring her home. He had just admitted her to a local hospital. He said she was really depressed, and asked that I talk with her when I had an opportunity. I assured him that I would go right then.

Marie told me of her shocking experience in the New England hospital, how awfully depressed she was, and with tears streaming down her face said, "It's a terrible thing when you face the reality of death."

"Marie, are you afraid of death?"

"Yes, I am."

Marie and Ted had been active members of their church for many years, but I had to ask her an important question.

"Marie, do you know for sure that you are going to Heaven?"

"I hope so."

"That's not good enough. You can know. You can know that you are going to Heaven just as surely as you know that you are a married woman."

I opened the Word of God to Marie that day, and I showed her what God had shown to me long before when He was seeking me:

These things have I written unto you that believe on the name of the Son of God; that ye may know that ye have eternal life, and that ye may believe on the name of the Son of God (1 John 5:13).

" 'These things' are the Bible, and God is the author of the Bible, and He wants us to know for sure that we have eternal life. For instance, I have had life insurance policies that your husband, Ted, sold me, and I believe the validity of those policies, but this is even more valid. This is not a contract or business with men; this is the Word of God. These things are written that you might know that you have eternal life." And I showed her that God loved her, Marie, so much that He gave His only begotten Son (John 3:16), and that if she believed in Him, she would not perish but have everlasting life.

I showed Marie the need for God to give His Son. Even when we try to do the best we can (and this lady certainly was not a "down and out" person, but was a fine, moral lady), we cannot attain to God's high standard. God says we all have sinned and come short of the glory of God (Romans 3:23), and He says "the soul that sinneth, it shall die" (Ezekiel 18:4). But God wasn't willing that any should perish. He loved us so much that He gave His Son, and Jesus Christ took care of our sin debt when He died on the cross.

Who his own self bare our sins in his own body on the tree,
that we, being dead to sins, should live unto righteousness:
by whose stripes ye were healed (1 Peter 2:24).

I showed Marie that Jesus died and was buried, but He arose and is alive today. Furthermore, if she would receive God's gift, Jesus Christ, she would have eternal life. I told her how she could become a child of God (John 1:12). I showed her that if she believed on the Son of God she would have the witness in herself (1 John 5:10). She would know when it happened, where it happened.

And this is the record, that God hath given to us eternal
life, and this life is in his Son (1 John 5:11).

How long is eternal life? Forever. And this life is in His Son.
He that hath the Son hath life, and he that hath not the Son
of God hath not life (1 John 5:12).

"Marie, on January 7, 1942, I received Jesus. I have the Son. I have eternal life. Now, I'm not asking you when you joined something, or even when you received someone; I'm asking when did you receive Jesus Christ?"

Marie looked at me and said: "I haven't."

"Would you like to?" And there in that hospital bed Marie received Christ as her Savior and Lord. She has the Son; she has eternal life.

Her husband came into the room about ten minutes later. Marie wasn't depressed any more. Her face was radiant and full of joy.

She said, "Ted, I have just received Jesus Christ. I am born again. I have eternal life."

Then I showed Ted what I had shown her. Ted, also, received Jesus as his Lord and Savior.

They know that Marie is sick. They don't know how long she will live; **but they do know that they will spend eternity in Heaven together!**

Chapter 21

GOD SAVES JANITORS TOO!

I went to the Christian high school where we were conducting a Bible Training Institute and where I was the teacher in personal evangelism. I planned to teach that night how to introduce people to Jesus Christ. As I walked into the classroom I met the elderly man who was supplementing his meager Social Security income by working as the night janitor. We greeted each other and got to talking.

"Bill, do you mind answering a question for me?"

"What's that, Pastor Orr?"

"If someone were to ask you what a Christian is, what would you say?"

"Well, I would say that a Christian is one who goes to church."

"Yes, a Christian should do that. You go to church regularly, Bill?"

"Yes."

"But what is a Christian?"

"Someone who reads his Bible."

"Yes, a Christian should read his Bible. Do you, Bill?"

"Yes, I read my Bible."

"That's good. But what is a Christian?"

"Well, people who pray."

"Christians certainly should pray. Do you pray, Bill?"

"Yes, I'm a man of prayer."

"But what is a Christian?"

"Oh, one who treats his family right."

"That's right. But what is a Christian?"

"People who treat their neighbors right."

"Yes, that is right too; but, Bill, what is a Christian?"

Bill looked at me and said: "Well, that's what a Christian is."

"No, Bill, that's what a Christian does. You still haven't told me what a Christian is."

Bill looked puzzled, and I asked if he would mind if I showed him just four verses in the Bible. He said he wouldn't mind. I turned to Romans 3:23:

For all have sinned, and come short of the glory of God.

"How many have sinned, Bill?"

"All."

"Does that mean me?"

"Yes."

"Does that mean you, too?"

"Yeah."

"Well then, we are all sinners. Right?"

"Right."

Then I turned to Romans 6:23:

For the wages of sin is death; but the gift of God is eternal life through Jesus Christ our Lord.

"Bill, you get paid for being a janitor here. I get paid for being a minister. We work and deserve the pay or wage that we receive. But the verse we just read is bad news. God says there is a wage for sinning. We deserve that wage too because we have already agreed that we are sinners. But what is death? Physical death means separation. My father and mother died just ten months apart, and I miss them since we are separated. But spiritual death means separation from God. If we die in our sins we will be separated from God forever. But the verse doesn't end with the terrible knowledge that the wages of sin is death, it goes on to promise us that the gift of God is eternal life through Jesus Christ our Lord.

The gift of God . . . "Do you ever receive gifts, Bill?"

"Oh, yes."

"Do you have to pay for them?"

"No."

"No. If you had to pay for them they would not be gifts; they'd be purchases. Do you have to work for them?"

"No."

"Right. If you had to work for them they'd be wages. What do you have to do?"

"Why, just take them," Bill said.

"But it cost the one who gave you the gift something, didn't it?"

"Yes."

"Now the gift of God is eternal life. How long is that? Forever. And it's through Jesus Christ, our Lord." Then I showed him the third Scripture:

But as many as received him, to them gave he power to become the sons of God, even to them that believe on his name (John 1:12).

"Bill, if you received God's gift, Jesus Christ, what would you become?"

"A child of God."

"Then how many times would you be born?"

"Twice."

"When were you born the second time?"

"When I received Jesus Christ."

We turned then to the fourth Scripture and read:

Behold, I stand at the door, and knock: if any man hear my voice, and open the door, I will come in to him, and will sup with him, and he with me (Revelation 3:20).

I asked Bill if he had seen the painting of Jesus standing outside a closed door knocking on it, and he said that he had.

"Bill, you know that's where Jesus was in my life on January 7, 1942, when I realized that I needed to open the door and ask Him in. I knew that Jesus wanted to come in. He wanted to make me a child of God. Bill, Jesus is outside of your life's door, isn't He? Don't you want to ask Him to come in?"

"Yes, I do."

And that night, before my class in personal evangelism began, God's truth was put into practice. Bill became a child of God. The next week Bill brought his wife and son, and both of them received Christ.

Bill has gone on to Heaven. His wife and son still live. The son just recently was in a backslidden condition, but he has confessed his sins and come back to the Lord.

The Bible says:

But if our gospel be hid, it is hid to them that are lost: **In** whom the god of this world hath blinded the minds of them which believe not, lest the light of the glorious gospel of Christ, who is the image of God, should shine unto them (2 Corinthians 4:3-4).

Bill knew what a Christian does, but he really didn't know what a Christian is. **There are millions who do not know the joy of being a real Christian — be one in a million! Be different!**

Chapter 22

A TRACT TRAVELS TO INDIA

And Saul, yet breathing out threatenings and slaughter against the disciples of the Lord, went unto the high priest, And desired of him letters to Damascus to the synagogues, that if he found any of this way, whether they were men or women, he might bring them bound unto Jerusalem. And as he journeyed, he came near Damascus: and suddenly there shined round about him a light from heaven: And he fell to the earth, and heard a voice saying unto him, Saul, Saul, why persecutest thou me? And he said, Who art thou, Lord? And the Lord said, I am Jesus whom thou persecutest: it is hard for thee to kick against the pricks. And he trembling and astonished said, Lord, what wilt thou have me to do? And the Lord said unto him, Arise, and go into the city, and it shall be told thee what thou must do (Acts 9:1-6).

Our Lord Jesus commissioned His disciples — and the commission has never been changed — that we should go into all the world and disciple all nations, baptizing them in the name of the Father and of the Son and of the Holy Ghost (Matthew 28:19).

I had the God-given privilege of coming to know Christ as my Lord and Savior. Later, I was also privileged to write a tract: "I Was Too Bad For Heaven But Too Good For Hell."

The Bible Tract Fellowship in our city sends out samples of tracts all over the world, and in this sample kit are a few copies of my tract. Among other places, this kit has been sent to a mission in India. The rural people of India could not read or understand English, but a few people connected with a heathen festival could read English and so my tracts were given to them. One of the tracts got into the hands of a communist leader named Johu Reddy. Now Johu Reddy was a little "Saul of Tarsus." He had been born and raised in a Christian home, but his parents were killed in an automobile accident when Johu was 16 years of age. He was taken into a foster home and inducted into communism. After graduating from college, he became a communist leader and so remained for 31 years. He hated Christians and their beliefs. He burned untold numbers of Bibles. He beat and otherwise threatened Christians who distributed Christian literature. Wouldn't you know that somehow, some way, my personal tract would get into the hands of a communist.

As Johu read "I Was Too Bad For Heaven But Too Good for Hell," he realized that he was a sinner. He realized that the wages of sin was death, and that when he met his appointment with death (according to Hebrews 9:27), judgment would be upon him, and he would go to Hell.

Johu saw his need of a savior. He also became aware of the fact that God loved him and had given His Son as his sacrifice, and that Jesus Christ on the cross of Calvary suffered and died for his sins that he, Johu, might be reconciled to God.

Johu opened his heart and received Jesus Christ as his Lord and Savior. He followed the Lord in water baptism. His desire was to let Christ live out of his life. It was as if the Scripture quoted from Acts, above, had become a reality. What had happened to Saul of Tarsus also happened to Johu Reddy. Now instead of beating the Christians, he has joined them in proclaiming the gospel of Jesus Christ. He has been distributing Christian tracts. He has a deep burden that his people might also come to know Jesus Christ as their Lord and Savior.

There is none that understandeth, there is none that seeketh after God. They are all gone out of the way, they are together become unprofitable; there is none that doeth good, no, not one (Romans 3:11-12).

God seeks the sinner. Just as our first parents sinned and sought to avoid God, you'll remember it was God who came to them saying, "Adam, where art thou?" And through a gospel tract, a personal testimony, God was saying to one Johu Reddy in India: "Johu, where art thou?" God knew, of course, where Johu was, but He wanted Johu to realize where he was . . . a sinner lost, without God, without Christ, without a hope in this world. But now, Johu Reddy, a believer, called upon the name of the Lord and was gloriously saved. His life was transformed. He is now distributing Christian literature so that his own countrymen might come to the saving knowledge of Jesus Christ and share his joy.

Have you ever known that joy? If not, why don't you turn in your Bible and read John 3:3, John 3:5, and John 3:7 where Jesus teaches that you must be born again. Then read John 1:12 and receive Jesus Christ. Today you can be born again and become a child of God. It is wonderful that a simple little tract could travel to India to do its work; it is even more wonderful, wonderful beyond all words, that **the living Word of God, our Lord Jesus Christ, should travel all the way from Heaven to Calvary to give us life and assurance for all eternity!**

Chapter 23

"I NEED TO BE SAVED"

The Pharisees also came unto him, tempting him, and saying unto him, Is it lawful for a man to put away his wife for every cause? And he answered and said unto them, Have ye not read, that he which made them at the beginning made them male and female, And said, For this cause shall a man leave father and mother, and shall cleave to his wife: and they twain shall be one flesh? Wherefore they are no more twain, but one flesh. What therefore God hath joined together, let no man put asunder (Matthew 19:3-6).

Jesus is speaking here. He is giving confirmation and His approval to the account in Genesis where the Lord God said that it was not good for man to live alone. Therefore He caused the man to sleep, and He took one of his ribs and made a woman and brought the woman to the man.

Christian marriage is a beautiful thing! God does not sanction divorce. God is always for reconciliation no matter what the problems are. And sin does cause problems.

Lawrence and Emily Lance were happily married. They had three wonderful children. But tragedy came into their home; their little baby died.

At our Wednesday night prayer service a lady asked that this family be included in our prayers since they had just lost a dear little baby. We prayed. And the lady who had requested prayer went to visit the bereaved parents. She read to them from the book of Samuel how David's little child died also, and how it was revealed in the Word of God that, while David's child could not return to him, he could go to be with the child. Our lady asked Emily if she knew that she was going to Heaven when she died. Emily said that she did not, and our lady had the privilege of leading Emily to Jesus Christ. Emily made a valid decision and received Christ as her Lord and Savior.

The next day was Thanksgiving Day. I received a telephone call from Lawrence:

"Pastor, I know it's a holiday and you probably have company. But could you possibly come to my home? I would like to know that I am going to be with my baby also."

I went to their home. Lawrence made a decision. Later on, however, he said it was not a valid decision. He had not made a total commitment.

It was a wild, stormy night when Lawrence called me again several years later and asked if he could come to see me. He got to my home about ten o'clock that night and he was so frightened that his face was chalky white.

Lawrence was working out of town and was tempted to fall into gross sin. God the Holy Spirit had convicted him. He wasn't sure that he was saved, but he did know that what he was about to do was absolutely wrong in the sight of God.

"Pastor, I pretty near fell into gross sin. I need to be saved."

"Didn't you mean it when you asked Christ to come into your life?"

"I thought I meant it. But I guess I didn't, not really. But tonight I want Christ to save me not only from Hell, but from my sins and the power of sin. I do not want to be a servant of sin."

We read of God's love for him, of Jesus being born of a virgin and living a sinless life so that He was the perfect sacrifice when He died on the cross of Calvary for Lawrence's sin and thus enables a just and holy God to take Lawrence to Heaven. We read how Jesus arose from the grave and is alive today, and how He wants to come into our lives and live through us. We discussed how He has a plan for each life.

There in my study that night with tears dropping on the floor as we knelt together, Lawrence asked Jesus Christ to come into his life and be his Savior and Lord.

What a tremendous change took place in the life of this

young man. A tremendous change came into the home when Jesus took charge of his life.

Lawrence was just another sinner, as we all are. But he became a child of God through faith in Jesus Christ. He was no longer burdened with guilt and under the power of sin. He had the joyful knowledge that he was Heaven-born and Heaven bound.

And such were some of you.

Chapter 24

ROCK BAND LEADER LED TO CHRIST

Jimmy Green was a rock band leader and music composer. He also worked for an industry where one of our church ladies was the secretary, and she had an opportunity to witness to him. Some people don't seem to realize it, but every born-again Christian is a missionary and should witness to others.

But ye shall receive power, after that the Holy Ghost is come upon you: and ye shall be witnesses unto me both in Jerusalem, and in all Judaea, and in Samaria, and unto the uttermost part of the earth (Acts 1:8).

Some Christians are better witnesses than others, of course, and witnessing cannot be effective if done in our own power. Every Christian receives the power of the Holy Spirit and the Lord wants us to witness wherever we are . . . In Jerusalem, Judaea, Samaria, and in the uttermost parts of the earth. That includes our neighborhoods, schools, where we work, and wherever we are. It's like throwing a stone into a lake. The ripples in the water go out, and out, and farther out. The Lord wants our witness to spread in that same manner.

Linda was witnessing to Jimmy Green about what the Lord had done for her, and Jimmy was interested. But Linda one day confided:

"Pastor, I can get him up the tree, but I can't bring him down."

Soon afterward, Linda called again and excitedly told me that Jimmy wanted to talk to me and that he'd have an hour free about six o'clock that evening. It seemed that Jimmy's wife did not want him to "get religious" and learn more about the gospel. Since she was in the hospital that evening, Jimmy could visit with me between taking her to and from the hospital.

My son and his family, who lived about one hundred miles from us, had planned a special anniversary dinner for my wife and me. I had planned to spend the better part of the day with them, but I told Linda that if Jimmy sincerely wanted to talk with me I would certainly make myself available at the time he could come. I asked her to find out if he really was serious; otherwise, I wanted to spend the time with my children and grandchildren. She reported back that Jimmy was serious and would definitely come at the appointed time.

Linda had told me that Jimmy looked like a "hippy" and, sure enough, he came with his long hair and sandals that were so much a part of their fashion at that time.

I showed Jimmy from the Word of God that Jesus Christ came that he, Jimmy Green, might have life eternal; that he might know that he was going to Heaven; that he might have an abundant life here and now, life with direction and with purpose. I showed him how sin had separated him from God and from the rich life that God had planned for him, and I showed him also how he would go to a devil's hell unless he was reconciled to God.

God is not willing that anyone should perish. And, while the wages of sin is death, the gift of God is eternal life through Jesus Christ our Lord (Romans 6:23). I showed him in the Scriptures that Christ died for his sins, and He was buried, and arose again. Christ, the living Christ, is God's gift. I pointed out that you can't work for a gift or it would become a wage. You can't pay for a gift or it would become a purchase. A gift simply must be received or taken from the giver. And in order to receive eternal life, you must be willing to actually receive through faith God's gift of Jesus Christ. The moment you receive Jesus Christ you are born again:

But as many as received him, to them gave he power to become the sons of God, even to them that believe on his name (John 1:12).

"Pastor," Jimmy said with tears in his eyes, "I would like to receive Jesus Christ, but I can't today. I've got an engagement coming up — the biggest one I have ever had — and I know if I let Jesus Christ come into my life I'll be out of the rock band business because I know what goes on."

"Jimmy, let me ask you something. If I could give you, say, a million dollars if you would go out of the rock band business, would you reject such an offer?"

"Oh, no, I'd take the million dollars."

"Jimmy, which is the greater: eternal life or a million dollars?"

Jimmy got down on his knees and received Jesus Christ as his Lord and Savior.

Yes, the Lord did take Jimmy Green out of the rock band business. Now Jimmy, like Linda and other born-again Christians, is witnessing for Jesus Christ.

And such were some of you.

Chapter 25

GOD WORKS IN STRANGE WAYS

Steve objected to Bible reading in his home, especially to his children. Sometimes his wife, Janie, would go into the bedroom and lock the door to read from the Word of God to their two daughters. Obviously, they did not go to church anywhere because Steve would not allow that.

Their daughters belonged to their high school youth group that sponsored a Bible club. The youth group also had sporting and other "fun" activities, and on one occasion sponsored a "Volkswagen Push." The daughters asked permission to attend this event. Their father thought it sounded interesting and decided to go with them. Well, they had their "Push" and there was a champion. But, more importantly, they heard a gospel message too.

Steve noticed the following week at work that his engineering friend was wearing a little lapel pin which many at the Volkswagen Push had also worn.

"Were you at the Volkswagen Push?" Steve inquired.

"No, I wasn't able to be there," replied the engineer. But he used that opening to talk about the gospel. Since it was hot, summer-time weather, the engineer suggested that they take a ride in his air-conditioned car so he could tell Steve more about the Lord and his need of Him. When they returned to the factory where they worked, Steve received Jesus Christ as his Lord and Savior.

The engineer called me and told me that since Steve and his family lived in our area and needed to become active in a Bible-believing church, he thought it would be good for me to meet with Steve so I could invite him and his family to our church. Arrangements were made and at the appointed time we met at Steve's home.

"Janie," I greeted the wife and mother, "I'm sure you are happy about your husband's decision."

"I don't understand," she responded. "I don't know what you are talking about. What did he do?"

"Well, Steve has received Jesus Christ as his Lord and Savior. He has been born again."

Janie's eyes got big and she said, "I can't believe it. I don't believe this is real. Not my husband. He won't let us even read the Bible. He won't let us go to church."

"Then you are a saved person, Janie?"

"Oh, no. I'm not saved."

"Wouldn't you like to be?"

"I certainly would."

Janie was ready. How she rejoiced to read from the Word of God that God the Father loved her so much that He gave His only begotten Son; that the baby that was born in Bethlehem's manger was the Son that was given; that He grew up and walked the face of this earth and was totally without sin; and that He willingly laid down His life upon Calvary's cross:

... I lay down my life, that I might take it again. No man taketh it from me, but I lay it down of myself. I have power to lay it down, and I have power to take it again. This commandment have I received of my Father (John 10:17-18).

Janie saw that He laid down his life for her, that He died for her personal sins, every one of them. He suffered so that He might bring her to God. She realized that He is alive and is her gift from God. She received Him as her Lord and Savior.

Oh, what rejoicing there was in that home. Steve embraced his wife. Both of them were saved, and his one desire now was that their daughters would be saved also. But they were visiting away from home that night.

The next Sunday the whole family came to me and the girls said they wanted to make the same decision their parents had made. They, too, received Jesus as their Savior.

Now Steve, Janie, and their daughters are a vital part of a local Bible-believing church where they truly love and serve the

Lord Jesus.

Think it not strange that God in His great love could save a whole family!

Chapter 26

OUT OF DARKNESS INTO THE LIGHT

Behold, what manner of love the Father hath bestowed upon us, that we should be called the sons of God (1 John 3:1).

There is none that understandeth, there is none that seeketh after God (Romans 3:11).

Shirley had a learner's permit and should have had an experienced driver with her, but she didn't. Her car upset. One of our church men came along and helped get her car back on its wheels. She wanted to pay him, but he refused pay. Instead, he invited her to come to our church the following Sunday.

Shirley and her husband were active in a liberal church studying different religions. They studied about seven various religions and were quite confused as to the real truth. They didn't know for sure that they were saved.

They did visit our church the following Sunday. At the close of the service when I gave the invitation, Shirley raised her hand for prayer, but she did not come forward. Others did, and we spent some time counseling with them. My wife told me, though, that Shirley was still waiting to talk with me too.

"I don't know that I am going to Heaven," she told me, "and I really would like to know."

I showed Shirley and Lyle the Gospel of Jesus Christ and God's plan of salvation. I showed them in Romans 3:23 that all have sinned and come short of the glory of God; that we are sinners and God is a Holy God, a righteous God, and a just God, and He cannot condone sin; and He pronounces death on sinners (Romans 6:23). But the bad news isn't the end of the Scripture, for that same verse continues and tells us that "the gift of God is eternal life through Jesus Christ our Lord." We read in the third chapter of John that Jesus emphasized three times that we must be born again. We have had a natural birth, but we must have a spiritual birth. Jesus says we **must be born again.** Then I showed Shirley and Lyle how, by receiving Jesus as God's free gift, they could be born again and become children of God (John 1:12). Out in our church parking lot Shirley asked Christ to come into her life.

"Shirley, how many times have you been born?"

"Twice."

"And what did you become?"

"A child of God," she answered, looking at John 1:12.

"And when you die, where will you go?"

"I don't know."

"Wait a minute," I said. And we spent several minutes reading and re-reading from God's Word His promise of eternal life to whoever will receive Jesus Christ as their Lord and Savior. But Shirley didn't have assurance of salvation.

The Spirit of God then led us to show her Scriptures in First John:

He that believeth on the Son of God hath the witness in himself: he that believeth not God hath made him a liar; because he believeth not the record that God gave of His Son. And this is the record, that God hath given to us eternal life, and this life is in his Son. He that hath the Son hath life; and he that hath not the Son of God hath not life. These things have I written unto you that believe on the name of the Son of God; that ye may know that ye have eternal life, and that ye may believe on the name of the Son of God (1 John 5:10-13).

"Shirley, were you sincere when you asked Christ to come into your life?"

"I certainly was."

"God's Word says that 'he that believeth not God hath made him a liar.' You wouldn't call God a liar, would you?"

"Oh no. God couldn't lie."

"Shirley, did you ask Christ to come into your life?"

"Yes."

"Well, if you have the Son, then what do you have?"

"Life."

"What kind of life?"

"Eternal life."

Suddenly her eyes got big and tearful and she looked at Lyle and exclaimed: "Lyle! I have been born again. I know I have eternal life."

Lyle said he was confused. But with further counseling and prayer, he also received Jesus Christ as his Lord and Savior.

Two souls were born again. When they came to church that morning they didn't know they were lost. But when they left church that day they knew they were saved.

God works in mysterious ways His wonders to perform!

Chapter 27

STORMS CAN BE BLESSINGS

And straightway Jesus constrained his disciples to get into a ship, and to go before him unto the other side, while he sent the multitudes away. And when he had sent the multitudes away, he went up into a mountain apart to pray: and when the evening was come, he was there alone. But the ship was now in the midst of the sea, tossed with waves: for the wind was contrary (Matthew 14:22-24).

Contrary winds! Storms come into the lives of the saved and the unsaved alike. These were Jesus' disciples that were going through the storm. And sometimes storms are so scary. In Psalm 107 we are told of waves that "mount up to the heaven, they go down again to the depths: . . . They reel to and fro, and stagger like a drunken man, and are at their wit's end. Then they cry unto the Lord in their trouble, and he bringeth them out of their distresses." Many times the Lord allows trouble to come into our lives so that we are willing for Him to reach us. This was true of June and Bill.

June was a patient in a hospital and shared a semi-private room with one of our church ladies. While visiting our lady one Sunday afternoon, I was introduced to June and her husband Bill. June told me that she was to undergo surgery the next day, and she added: "Pastor, I am afraid."

I went over to her bedside and asked her what she was afraid of. She was apprehensive about how serious her problem might be and that she might even die.

"If, or when, you die, because death comes to all of us sooner or later, do you know that you are going to Heaven?"

"No, I don't."

"What about you, Bill?"

"Well," he said, "that's a pretty difficult question to answer. I can't say that I know for sure."

"It's about as difficult as if I had asked you if you were married."

"Well, of course I know I'm married."

"How do you know that you are married?"

He looked at me and said, "Look, we got married in a church (and he named the date) and I'll never forget that."

"Yes, Bill, I know. It sounds like a foolish question. But you do know a time and a place where you made your vows to June. You promised: 'I, Bill, take you, June, to be my wedded wife, to have and to hold from this day forward, for better, for worse, for richer, for poorer, in sickness and in health, to love and to cherish, till death us do part.' You need to do the very same thing with Jesus. Just as you and June fell in love and gave yourselves to each other, God the Father loved you so much that He gave you His Son. God the Son loved you so much that He went to the cross of Calvary and gave His life for your sins. Jesus is standing outside the door of your life and He wants to come in:

Behold, I stand at the door, and knock: if any man hear my voice, and open the door, I will come in to him . . . (Revelation 3:20).

And I showed them John 1:12 which assured them that if they would receive Jesus, they would become the children of God.

"June, would you like to receive Christ today? Are you willing by faith, forsaking all, to ask Jesus Christ to come into your life and be your Lord and Savior?"

Bill wanted to receive Christ also. And as I held June's and Bill's hands, I heard them pray:

"Dear God, I thank you for loving me and I thank you for giving your Son. And dear Jesus, I thank you for coming to my heart's door. I open my heart and I want you to come in and take over my life. I want you to be my Lord and my Savior."

And we prayed together and rejoiced. I looked at June and the beautiful smile on her face reflected perfect peace. She wasn't afraid any more.

Bill and June have been coming to church and their lives have been transformed by the power of the gospel of Jesus Christ. They are an active part of the church. The "storm" that day when June was facing surgery affected both husband and wife because they were no more twain, but were one in marriage. No storm is too great for Jesus Christ.

And in the fourth watch of the night Jesus went unto them, walking on the sea. And when the disciples saw him walking on the sea, they were troubled, saying, It is a spirit; and they cried out for fear. But straightway Jesus spake unto them, saying, Be of good cheer; it is I; be not afraid. And Peter answered him and said, Lord, if it be thou, bid me come unto thee on the water. And he said, Come. And when Peter was come down out of the ship, he walked on the water, to go to Jesus. But when he saw the wind boisterous, he was afraid; and beginning to sink, he cried, saying, Lord, save me. And immediately Jesus stretched forth his hand, and caught him, and said unto him, O thou of little faith, wherefore didst thou doubt? And when they were come into the ship, the wind ceased (Matthew 14:25-32).

I will never forget June and Bill in that hospital room. How good it was that a "storm" came into their lives because, through it, they heard the gospel. They believed the gospel, and they called upon the name of the Lord.

And such were some of you.

Chapter 28

THE MAN WHO WANTED TO BE AN AMBASSADOR

Horace was an aide to a Representative of the United States Congress, and he was quite concerned about the spread of communism throughout the world. He had been talking with some of my relatives who suggested that he pay me a visit. This he did.

While I was aware of much of what he was concerned about, other information which he gave me was astounding. This good-looking young man was really burdened. He told me that he really loved his country, he loved God, and he wanted his life to count for something.

"Horace, I notice that your love for your country comes first, your love for God comes second, and a worthwhile life is third in your desires and priorities. I believe that the first two are in reverse order for me. First of all, I love God, then my family, and then my country."

And I related to him my personal testimony. I did not know that I was lost and I had never heard the gospel of Jesus Christ until some time after I was grown and had been an active member of our church. Horace was interested.

I showed him in the Bible that "There is none that understandeth, there is none that seeketh after God" (Romans 3:11). I remarked about the coincidences of his doing business with my relative who referred him to me, how unusual it was that I would be home at just the time he came and we would have an opportunity to visit, and I firmly believed that God wanted to do real business with him.

I showed him in the Word of God that God loved him so much that He gave His only begotten Son (John 3:16). I explained how that was necessary because we have all sinned and come short of the glory of God (Romans 3:23). We read God's pronouncement that the wages of sin is death but the gift of God is eternal life through Jesus Christ our Lord (Romans 6:23). Then we turned to where Jesus said, "I am come that they might have life, and that they might have it more abundantly" (John 10:10). Our sins separate us from God and from the abundant life that God planned for us, but Jesus died for our sins and arose again, and He wants to come into each of our lives.

Horace saw his need. He bowed beside me and asked Jesus Christ to come into his life and be his Savior and Lord. Oh, how he rejoiced in his salvation and the way that God had spoken to him.

"Horace, what are you doing tonight?"

"I have an appointment with my doctor, but what did you have in mind?"

"We have a Wednesday night prayer service, and I thought perhaps you'd come along with me and give your testimony."

"Oh," he said, "that's more important than going to the doctor."

Horace had dinner with us and went along to our service. I'll never forget his testimony:

"This morning I was a sinner on my way to Hell. I stopped at your Pastor's house and shared my concern about the spread of communism, my love for our country, and how I don't want it to go down the drain. And then Pastor Orr shared with me what Jesus Christ did for him, and what Jesus has done and wants to do for me. Today I received Christ as my Savior and as my Lord.

"As a young man, I've had one consuming desire: to be an ambassador to some foreign country for the United States. This afternoon, God made me an ambassador for Jesus Christ!"

Horace's testimony brought to my mind the following:

Now then we are ambassadors for Christ, as though God did beseech you by us: we pray you in Christ's stead, be ye reconciled to God. For he hath made him to be sin for us, who knew no sin; that we might be made the righteousness of God in him (2 Corinthians 5:20-21).

In that chapter of Second Corinthians, God gave us the ministry of reconciliation (verse 18), committed unto us the word of reconciliation (verse 19), and made us his ambassadors (verse 20).

Horace was right. Along with his salvation, God made him an ambassador for Jesus Christ!

Chapter 29

"WHAT IS THE GREATEST THING THAT EVER HAPPENED TO YOU?"

This is a question a friend of mine often asked as he was getting acquainted with strangers. One young man told him the greatest thing that ever happened to him was when he made the varsity football team for Notre Dame. Another responded that it was when his wife agreed to marry him. To another, it was when a doctor congratulated him upon the birth of his baby boy. So many various answers were given by different people to that question.

I would like to share with you the greatest thing that ever happened to me. I was what you might call an "up and outer" instead of a "down and outer." I was placed on the cradle roll of our church when I was three years old, and I grew up in the church through the primary, junior high, senior high, and adult departments of our Sunday School. I was very active in our church. I was youth director, Sunday School teacher and was on the church board of deacons. I edited the church newspaper. I played on the church's baseball and basketball teams. I attended all of the services on Sunday morning, Sunday night and Wednesday night. And I was quite happy!

The District Superintendent of our denomination came to our church to spearhead a movement to help young men go into the ministry who might not otherwise be financially able to go. My wife and I were on one of the solicitation teams. This elderly man met with us and related his own personal testimony.

He told us that when he went to college to study law he made the varsity football team, and one of the football players took him to church where he said he was "converted." He told us that he knew he was going to Heaven when he died. I became very angry when I heard him say that. I nudged my wife and said: "Who does he think he is? I've got questions for him." My wife urged me to keep quiet, and I did. But going home that night I was still angry and had to pick on someone, so I picked on my wife.

"What did you think of Dr. Schwartz tonight?"

"I thought he was excellent."

"So did I. An excellent braggart. He said when he dies he knows that he is going to Heaven."

"What's wrong with that?"

"Aw, come on, Millie. Who would have the audacity to say that they are good enough to go to Heaven?"

"Well," Millie said, "I think he knows."

"Well, let me ask you a question. If you were to die tonight, do you know for sure that you would go to Heaven? Don't give me an 'I think so' or 'I hope so' answer. This man said he knew."

Millie began to cry.

"Jack, if I died tonight, I would go to Hell."

"What are you talking about? You're a good wife, a good mother, a good church worker."

"You don't make any sense, Jack," Millie interrupted. "You get mad at Dr. Schwartz because he knows he's going to Heaven, and you get mad at me because I know I'm going to Hell. Think, man, there are only two places to go."

I had to agree with her that there were only two places to spend eternity: Heaven or Hell. I thought religion was a dumb thing to argue about, but I laid awake that night. I started to evaluate my life. I wondered why I was active in my church and just what my church membership really meant. I didn' know. I determined that I would attempt to find out the nex day.

I was an assistant manager in a chain drugstore, but I hac the following morning off. I told my wife I was going to see ou pastor. If anyone could know for sure he would spend eternity ir Heaven, that surely would be the greatest thing anyone coul know.

I began to walk the twelve blocks to the church so I could collect my thoughts. En route I would pass a Lutheran church, a United Brethren church, a Jewish synagogue, and two Catholic churches. I decided I would stop and ask each clergyman what the way to Heaven was. The first one wasn't at home. Then I thought I was just emotionally upset and I'd go home and forget the whole thing. But I couldn't get Millie's statement out of my mind: "Think, man, there are only two places to go. You get mad at Dr. Schwartz for going to Heaven and you get mad at me for going to Hell."

To my amazement, Millie was out when I got home. I know now that God worked it that way, otherwise I would have been too proud to do what I did. I got on my knees at the sofa and I prayed, "Oh God, if there is any way of knowing that you are going to Heaven, please let me know." And I felt impressed to get my Bible. When I opened it I began reading in First John, chapter five. Imagine my excitement when I read verse 13:

These things have I written unto you that believe on the name of the Son of God; that ye may know that ye have eternal life, and that ye may believe on the name of the Son of God (1 John 5:13).

What things? The Bible! I was astounded. There I was, praying that if there was any way to know, that God would show me, and here in the Bible, the Word of God, He was showing me how I could know. Now I know that it was the Spirit of God that directed my reading to the Epistle to the Romans next, and I read aloud Romans 3:11.

There is none that understandeth, there is none that seeketh after God.

I argued a bit with God about that. Didn't my mother put me on the cradle roll when I was a tiny infant? Didn't I grow up in the church, serving in many capacities? But then I realized that I didn't even choose the church. I didn't ask God whom I should marry. I didn't ask God's direction for any part of my life. I always called the plays. And I realized that it was God who had this man testify. It was God who had me searching the Scriptures right then. It was God who was seeking after me. Then I read:

For all have sinned, and come short of the glory of God (Romans 3:23).

I knew that I surely wasn't as good as God so I must be included in the word "all". Then I saw the penalty for my sin:

For the wages of sin is death; but the gift of God is eternal life through Jesus Christ our Lord (Romans 6:23).

I didn't really know what that meant. I was convicted. I knew that if I died I was going to Hell but I didn't know how to escape.

And as it is appointed unto men once to die, but after this the judgment (Hebrews 9:27).

This was not at all reassuring!

Later, when I did consult my pastor, he gave me a book on Bishop Francis Warren's conversion. As a little boy about twelve years old, the book related, Francis Warren prayed that he would be converted during the two weeks of meetings being held in his church; if not, he just wouldn't go to church any more. On Saturday before the meetings closed on Sunday, John 3:16 was made real and vital to his heart. He substituted his name for the words "the world" and saw that God so loved him, Francis Warren, that He gave His only begotten son for him. And I suddenly saw that too. Jesus died for me, Jack Orr. He paid the penalty for my sin. Then I followed up on a further reference:

For I delivered unto you first of all that which I also received, how that Christ died for our sins according to the scriptures; and that he was buried, and that he rose again the third day according to the scriptures (1 Corinthians 15:3-4).

I had known this as an historical fact. I believed the virgin birth, the death, burial, and resurrection of Jesus Christ. I knew all that, but this time it was personal. I realized that Jesus died for my sins. I knew that He was alive.

Then I went back and read the whole context in the third chapter of John. It told me about Nicodemus and how he came to Jesus by night. Nicodemus told Jesus that he knew Him to be a teacher who had come from God, "for no man can do these miracles that thou doest, except God be with him" (John 3:2).

Jesus answered and said unto him, Verily, verily, I say unto thee, Except a man be born again, he cannot see the kingdom of God (John 3:3).

I put my Bible down, wondering how a person could be born

twice. How could a person be born again? And I picked up my Bible and read further. Nicodemus was just as puzzled as I. He asked Jesus that very same question.

Jesus explained to Nicodemus, and to me, that he was born the first time in the flesh . . . a physical birth . . . and he must be born again of the Spirit.

And as Moses lifted up the serpent in the wilderness, even so must the Son of Man be lifted up: That whosoever believeth in him should not perish, but have eternal life. For God so loved the world, that he gave his only begotten Son, that whosoever believeth in him should not perish, but have everlasting life (John 3:14-16).

In that moment the Spirit of God made me understand and realize that Jesus took care of my sin problem, that He died for my sins that He might bring me to God. I looked up one more Scriptural reference:

But as many as received him, to them gave he power to become the sons of God, even to them that believe on his name (John 1:12).

I knew that I needed Christ in my life. I knelt and prayed:

"Oh, Dear God, I thank you for loving me and giving your Son. Lord Jesus, I thank you for coming from Heaven to earth and suffering and dying for my sins. I'm glad you are alive, and right now I want you to please come into my life, take over my life, and be my Savior and be my Lord." I meant that, and so did God.

I read John 1:12 again and knew that I had received Jesus. I called to my wife: "Millie, I am born again!"

And such were some of you. If you have never made that all-important decision, why don't you do it today? You'll never regret it. **It is the greatest thing that ever happened to me.**

Chapter 30

"A WOMAN SET FREE

The Bible tells us that three things will happen if we are really Heaven-born and Heaven-bound.

The first thing is:

Behold, what manner of love the Father hath bestowed upon us, that we should be called the sons of God (1 John 3:1).

"Behold, what manner of love . . ." If a person is going to Heaven it is only because God loves him. "For God so loved the world . . ." (John 3:16), and, "All we like sheep have gone astray; we have turned every one to his own way; and the Lord hath laid on him the iniquity of us all" (Isaiah 53:6). If we want to see the love of God, we must go to Calvary and there see that Christ died for our sins. What manner of love, indeed!

The second thing is:

Beloved, now are we the sons of God . . . (1 John 3:2).

Notice the word "now" in that verse. "Now" is the key word. There has to be a time and a place when one becomes a child of God. In John 3:3, Jesus declares that, "Except a man be born again, he cannot see the kindgom of God." In John 3:5, Jesus states, "Except a man be born of water and of the Spirit, he cannot enter into the kingdom of God." And in John 3:7, Jesus tells us, "Marvel not that I said unto thee, Ye must be born again." There must be a time, there has to be a second birthday, when we receive Jesus Christ as our Lord and our Savior.

And the third thing is:

Whosoever is born of God doth not commit (practice) sin (1 John 3:9).

Our whole lifestyle is changed. Oh, we'll still sin . . . inadvertently and unwillingly . . . but we will not practice sin.

I had led to the Lord some relatives of a lady who had many problems, and it was my privilege to talk with her about being born again. She made a profession and even came to our church. One night she called me for an appointment to come for counseling, at which time she told me about her personal life. She knew and was convicted of wrong-doing in her life and, therefore, doubted that she was really saved. We re-read 1 John 3:9 and agreed that it was unlikely that her profession had been an earnest act of repentance of sin and a sincere turn-about to follow Jesus as her Lord and Savior.

We read other Scriptures again: God so loved her that He gave His only begotten Son (John 3:16). God did not want her to perish, and Christ died for her sins — not some of her sins, or most of them, but all of them. Amy became aware of this great truth. And she knew that even though Christ paid her sin debt by dying at Calvary, He arose on the third day, and He is alive now and forever more. And then we read that wonderful verse in John:

But as many as received him, to them gave he power to become the sons of God, even to them that believe on his name (John 1:12).

"Amy, did you really mean it? Did you ever really receive Christ by faith?" And I spelled it out: F-A-I-T-H, forsaking all I take Him. "Did you ever sincerely see your need for being saved, not only from going to Hell, but being saved from your sins now? Jesus wants to come into your life now and take over the management of your life and save you from the power of sin."

"I think I know my problem," Amy responded. "I made an intellectual decision. I believed all about Jesus, but I never meant it with my heart and soul. I really do want to receive Christ as my Lord and Savior."

We knelt in prayer, thanking God for showing Amy that she was a sinner and unable to live the Christian life unless Jesus

Christ became her Savior and lived through her as her **Lord and Master**. We thanked Jesus for coming from Heaven to earth **to** suffer and die for all of her sins. We told Jesus how thankful **we** were that He is alive and Amy asked Jesus Christ to come **into** her life and do for her what she could not do **for** herself . . . make her a new person, a child of God . . . and **we** thanked Him for doing it.

Joy flooded her soul. Amy knew that she indeed had **been** born again.

Therefore if any man be in Christ, he is a new creature: old
things are passed away; behold, all things are become new
(2 Corinthians 5:17).

Amy's life was completely transformed by the power of **God**. This sin that had gripped her and was pulling her down, this **sin** that she could not gain victory over, was overcome by her **new** life in Christ. He set her free. **She now enjoys the abundant life that Jesus Christ alone can give.**

Chapter 31

VICTORY IN DEATH

Robert and Jane were in love. They came to my office for pre-marital counseling. I explained to them out of the Word of God what Christian marriage really is.

We began in the Book of Genesis. God said it was not good for man to live alone, so He caused Adam to sleep and took from Adam a rib and made a woman, a helpmeet, and He brought the woman to the man and said for this cause "shall a man leave his father and his mother, and shall cleave unto his wife" (See Genesis 2:18-25).

I reminded Bob and Jane of the terrible divorce statistics of this present time. This, of course, is not God's intention. And I told them that if their proposed marriage was of God, God was bringing Jane to Bob. And I showed them how this teaching was confirmed by our Lord in Matthew 19. Then we looked in Ephesians 5, where the Apostle Paul compares marriage with the mystical union which subsists between Christ and His Church.

"Your wedding is something like when you get saved," I told them. "For instance, Bob, the best man, and I will come in and stand in the front of the church. Then the bridesmaids come down the aisle. At the sound of the chimes, the bride and her father approach the altar. Jane, are you single or are you married?"

"Oh, we are still single at that point."

"That's right. Then we'll ask you your intentions. I'll say 'Bob, are you willing to leave your father and mother and

121

forsake all others and take Jane as your lawful wedded wife?'
And he'll say, 'I will.' Then I'll ask, 'Jane, are you willing to
leave your father and mother and forsake all others and take
Bob?' And she will say, 'I will.' But you are still single because
you haven't made your vows.

"Then I ask: 'Who giveth this woman to this man?' And your
father will say: 'Her mother and I.' Now, we're getting down to
the essence of it.

"I, Bob, take thee, Jane, to be my wedded wife from this day
forward, for better, for worse, for richer, for poorer, in sickness
and in health, till death us do part.

"Jane hasn't made her vow yet, so you're still single. But
then Jane says: 'I, Jane, take thee, Robert, to be my wedded
husband from this day forward, for better, for worse, for richer,
for poorer, in sickness and in health, till death us do part." Then
it's my privilege to pronounce you man and wife. You're
married.

"Bob, if anyone asked you after that if you are married, you
wouldn't say you guessed so or you hoped so. No, of course not.
You know you are married. You know a time and a place where
you made your marriage vows."

I asked Jane if she knew a time and a place where she had
received Jesus Christ. Jane told me her testimony.

When I asked Bob a similar question, tears were already
running down his cheeks. "No, Pastor, I've never made such a
decision."

I told Bob of Jesus' love for him, how He died for his sins,
how He lives forevermore and wants to come into each person's
life. I asked Bob if he would like to open his life's door to Jesus
and ask Him to come in.

"Yes, oh yes, I would. I do want Jesus to come into my life."

We knelt in prayer and, according to the Word of God,
Robert became a child of God. Robert sincerely meant his
invitation to Christ, and God does not, cannot, lie, so Robert
was born again.

With joyful hearts we went on to discuss their responsibilities in a Christian marriage. God wants our homes to be a
little Heaven on earth. The wife is a type of the Church:

Wives, submit yourselves unto your own husbands, as unto
the Lord. For the husband is the head of the wife, even as

122

Christ is the head of the church: and he is the saviour of the body. Therefore as the church is subject unto Christ, so let the wives be to their own husbands in every thing (Ephesians 5:22-24).

Then I showed Bob his responsibilities:

Husbands, love your wives, even as Christ also loved the church, and gave himself for it (Ephesians 5:25).

Bob and Jane recognized their responsibilities. It was a beautiful wedding, and they had a lovely life together for just a little over a year. Then tragedy hit. Bob was killed in an automobile accident.

I remember conducting that memorial service for Bob where one of his best friends was a pall bearer. At the conclusion of the service, this friend, John, responded to the invitation to accept Christ as his Savior. All of Bob's family and friends had been well aware of the change that salvation had brought to his life. Now his death was impressing them with their need to hear and obey the Gospel. After the service, John introduced me to his girl friend, Margie, and she also received Jesus Christ.

As I looked at Jane, she was rejoicing. Oh, she and all Bob's family and friends had suffered a great loss in his death, but she knew that God was being glorified and that Bob was already present with the Lord. God's grace was sufficient for all her needs (as promised in 2 Corinthians), and Jane was a tremendous testimony to **the saving power of Jesus Christ.**

Chapter 32

FAITH IS THE VICTORY

We were invited into the home of a young couple to talk with another young couple about believer's baptism. We read in Matthew 28 where Jesus commanded His disciples to "teach all nations, baptizing them in the name of the Father, and of the Son, and of the Holy Ghost; Teaching them to observe all things whatsoever I have commanded you . . ."

I asked the young man to share his testimony. He told us how he had received Christ as his Savior just the past Friday as a man witnessed to him in his car. Now he and his wife stated they wanted to go all the way with the Lord. I asked the wife, Teressa, how long she had been saved. She said, "I am not."

We opened the Word of God to show her that she needed to be saved first of all and then she could follow the Lord in baptism. We pointed out how she was born in sin and was a sinner by nature and by practice, and was in need of the Savior. Even though God is holy and just and righteous, and cannot look upon sin, He still loves the sinner and is not willing that any should perish. We showed her in the Word of God how God's love was so great that Jesus Christ died in her place, and that He is alive again and wants to come into her life and be her Savior if she sincerely repents of her sin and asks Him to save her. I asked her if she would like to ask Him into her life. She said she would like to, but she would rather wait and do it when she got home. I was afraid her reluctance might cause her to put off such a decision indefinitely.

"Why don't you call me from home after you have asked

Jesus to be your Savior?"

"We don't have a telephone."

"Then perhaps on your way to work in the morning you could call me. I really am interested in your welfare, and this decision will be the most important one in your life."

The following morning Teressa called me. I was so happy to hear her voice. "You got saved!"

"Well, no, I didn't."

"Didn't you do it? Didn't you ask Jesus to come into your life and be your Savior?"

"Yes, I did, but I didn't get saved. Nothing happened."

Teressa had a problem that many others have. They look for an emotional feeling or experience instead of simply trusting God's promise. For example, you can turn in your Bible to John and read:

Now after two days he departed thence, and went into Galilee. For Jesus himself testified, that a prophet hath no honour in his own country. Then when he was come into Galilee, the Galilaeans received him, having seen all the things that he did at Jerusalem at the feast: for they also went unto the feast. So Jesus came again into Cana of Galilee, where he made the water wine. And there was a certain nobleman, whose son was sick at Capernaum. When he heard that Jesus was come out of Judaea into Galilee, he went unto him, and besought him that he would come down, and heal his son: for he was at the point of death. Then said Jesus unto him, Except ye see signs and wonders, ye will not believe (John 4:43-48).

Now this nobleman had a problem. His son was at the point of death. Being a nobleman, he probably had already tried everything possible to have his son healed. Then he heard that Jesus had come into Cana and, undoubtedly, he had heard of Jesus performing many miracles. He came to Jesus and requested: "Sir, come down ere my child die."

Now the nobleman probably thought that Jesus would touch him or go to his house and touch his son, but Jesus simply spoke:

Jesus saith unto him, Go thy way; thy son liveth. And the man believed the word that Jesus had spoken unto him, and he went his way. And as he was now going down, his servants met him, and told him, saying, Thy son liveth. Then enquired he of them the hour when he began to amend. And they said unto him, Yesterday at the seventh hour the fever left him. So the father knew that it was at the same hour, in the which Jesus said unto him, Thy son liveth, and himself believed, and his whole house (John 4:50-53).

The nobleman was looking for a sign, but he believed Jesus when He spoke. Teressa was looking for a sign also, or some inner feeling, but she, too, must take Jesus at His word.

"Teressa, you say that you asked Christ to come into your life?"

"Yes, I did."

"Did you really mean it?"

"I did. I meant it with all my heart."

"Teressa, listen to this:

But as many as received him, to them gave he power to become the sons of God, even to them that believe on his name (John 1:12).

"Teressa, did you receive Jesus? Did you sincerely ask Him into your heart and life, to forgive your sins, and to be your Lord and Savior?"

"I did."

"Can God lie?"

"No."

We read John 1:12 again. "Did you receive Jesus, Teressa?"

"Yes."

"Then what did you become?"

"A child of God." And she began to cry for joy. "I am born again!"

"Teressa, when were you born again?"

"Just now."

"No, not just now. When did you ask Christ to come into your life?"

"Pastor Orr, when I got inside the door of our home last night I fell on my knees and I asked Christ to come into my life and save me."

"Then when were you born again?"

"Last night when I received Jesus Christ as my Lord and
127

Savior."

Thank God, our salvation is not based on a feeling which we may have one day and not have another time. Our salvation is based on the factual truth of God's holy Word. And we need to know God's truth, believe it, and obey it.

Chapter 33

THIS MAN FOUND NEW LIFE

God speaks about the stormy wind in Psalms 107 and compares it with the trials of our lives.

Man that is born of a woman is of few days, and full of trouble (Job 14:1)

They mount up to the heaven, they go down again to the depths: their soul is melted because of trouble. They reel to and fro, and stagger like a drunken man, and are at their wit's end (Psalms 107:26-27).

Many of us have been at "wit's end corner". But God is never at His wit's end because the Scripture continues:

Then they cry unto the Lord in their trouble, and he bringeth them out of their distresses. He maketh the storm a calm, so that the waves thereof are still (Psalms 107:28-29).

One of the greatest storms that we have experienced concerned the hydrogen bubble at the Three Mile Island Nuclear Plant. The warning of possible evacuation was given. First, the people within a five-mile radius would be evacuated, then those within the ten-mile radius. We were within that ten-mile radius. I'll never forget going one morning to the bank to take care of a regular transaction and finding lines of people before every teller. People had shopping bags and briefcases and they were all drawing out money. People were panicky. Some said that if the bubble burst we would lose everything we had, and that people would not be able to go into that area again for hundreds of years. It was interesting to me to observe the

129

attitudes of the Christians and those of the non-Christians.

When I entered my home upon returning from the bank, I could hear the telephone ringing. The caller said his name was Anderson.

"Pastor Orr, I was only ever in your church one time. I'm scared. I have a shotgun and I am going to take my life. I've read in the Bible where it says, 'Come unto me, all ye that labor and are heavy laden, and I will give you rest.' Doesn't that mean that I will go to Heaven?"

"No! Whatever you do, don't take your life. Listen, God has a wonderful, wonderful story for you to hear." And I related to that worried man how God loved him so much that He sent His Son into the world; that the baby that was born in Bethlehem's manger was the fulfillment of Isaiah 9:6, "For unto us a child is born, unto us a son is given . . ." Jesus came into this world not to be ministered unto, but to minister and to give His life a ransom for many. On the cross of Calvary Jesus Christ became his, Mr. Anderson's, substitute, his sacrifice for sin. Because we are all sinners, and the wages of sin is death, God provided a plan for our salvation. He gave His only begotten Son. Jesus provided for our salvation when He paid the price for our sins by dying on the cross. But Jesus arose again after three days, according to the Scriptures. God's gift to sinful man is eternal life through Jesus Christ our Lord.

I reminded Mr. Anderson that we can't work for a gift. We can't pay for a gift. The only way to receive a gift is to appropriate it, or simply claim and take it. It cost the giver something, but for Mr. Anderson it was free. In this case, God the Father was the giver: He gave His only begotten Son. It cost God the Son His life when Jesus came down from Heaven to earth and gave His life on Calvary's cross. It is up to us — Mr. Anderson, you, and me — to take the gift of eternal life.

That day on the telephone, Mr. Anderson prayed a prayer of thanksgiving for God's unspeakable gift of love, and he received Jesus Christ as his Lord and Savior. He was rejoicing. He didn't take his life. He found new life — eternal life.

The bubble did not burst and we were spared much trouble, expense, and possibly death. But Jesus Christ is coming again "in the twinkling of an eye" and there won't be time then for any evacuation because "the dead in Christ shall rise first·

Then we which are alive and remain shall be caught up together with them in the clouds, to meet the Lord in the air: and so shall we ever be with the Lord" (1 Thessalonians 4:16-17).

This is not a "bubble" or a possibility: this is factual. It will take place. But Mr. Anderson need no longer live in fear because he is now a child of God through Jesus Christ. **And, you, too, can be a child of God.**

Chapter 34

HE THOUGHT HE HAD NO NEED

He was a fine, upright, morally good fellow who only had one problem: **He was not saved.**

We had the privilege of sowing the seed in Carl's life, and God gave the increase. Carl and his wife were one very fine couple. His wife was saved and had a real burden for her husband. He was a wonderful fellow who simply did not see his need. I remember one day the Christian Business Men had a meeting and Dave Boyer, the well-known Gospel singer, was to sing and give his testimony. I invited Carl to attend that dinner meeting with me to hear Dave. On our way home I asked Carl how he had enjoyed the concert. He said he had enjoyed it very much.

"Carl, have you ever received Christ? Have you ever made that most important decision?" (Dave had just told of his conversion from a life that was not so good.)

"To tell you the truth, Jack, I was never that kind of a person. I always tried to do the thing that was right. I belong to the church, I give to the church, I believe in God, I try to be a good husband, a good father. Honestly, I don't see where my need is."

It reminded me of a teaching of Jesus:

And he spake this parable unto certain which trusted in themselves that they were righteous, and despised others: Two men went up into the temple to pray; the one a Pharisee, and the other a publican. The Pharisee stood and prayed thus with himself, God, I thank thee, that I am not

133

as other men are, extortioners, unjust, adulterers, or even as this publican. I fast twice in the week, I give tithes of all that I possess. And the publican, standing afar off, would not lift up so much as his eyes unto heaven, but smote upon his breast, saying, God be merciful to me a sinner. I tell you, this man went down to his house justified rather than the other: for every one that exalteth himself shall be abased; and he that humbleth himself shall be exalted (Luke 18:9-14).

Here are two men, both praying. One of them was "good" and one was "bad". And, according to the Scriptures, the bad man was the one who was saved. And here was Carl, a good man, but lost.

While we continued our discussion in Carl's home that night, he said, "Jack, for your sake and for my wife's sake, I would like to make that decision, but I honestly don't see any need. And if I do it I will only be playing games."

"Well, don't play games, Carl. Don't play games."

In subsequent cottage prayer meetings preceding an evangelistic meeting we were planning, Carl was at the top of our prayer list. We were all praying that Carl would be convinced and convicted by the Holy Spirit to see his need for Jesus Christ to be his Savior.

One of our prayer meetings was scheduled to be held in the home of Carl and his wife. I told her that since Carl was at the top of our prayer list that he might be embarrassed if he were home that night. I asked if we should take him off our list for that night or have the meeting somewhere else. But she asked us to come on to their home and to leave Carl's name at the head of our prayer list.

When we arrived at the appointed time, there were quite a number of us gathered there. Carl greeted us with, "I believe Ethel has something to praise the Lord about."

"You tell them," Ethel said.

"I want you to know that this morning in my bedroom I got down on my knees and I received Christ as my Lord and Savior. I was saved this morning." And Carl shared with us some of the things that already had left his life. And we knew that his blessings had just begun. How we rejoiced!

You have been reading in previous chapters about, and

134

perhaps know personally, people who were down and out and knew that they were sinners in need of a Savior. But people who have the most difficulty in becoming aware of their needs are the morally good, upright, conscientious people like Carl and like the Pharisee we read about in Luke. But Jesus teaches in that parable that a "good" man can be lost and go to Hell and a "bad" man can be saved and go to Heaven. None of us can ever be good enough. There is only one way to Heaven and that is through faith in Jesus Christ.

He that hath the Son hath life; and he that hath not the Son of God hath not life (1 John 5:12).

The decision Carl made that morning made all the difference in his life and where he will spend eternity. **He awoke that morning without Christ in his life. He went to bed that night knowing that he had received Jesus Christ as his Savior for ever and ever.**

Chapter 35

THE GIRL MADE THE RIGHT DECISION

And a certain ruler asked him, saying, Good Master, what shall I do to inherit eternal life? And Jesus said unto him, Why callest thou me good? None is good, save one, that is, God. Thou knowest the commandments, Do not commit adultery, Do not kill, Do not steal, Do not bear false witness, Honour thy father and thy mother. And he said, All these have I kept from my youth up. Now when Jesus heard these things, he said unto him, Yet lackest thou one thing: sell all that thou hast, and distribute unto the poor, and thou shalt have treasure in heaven: and come, follow me. And when he heard this, he was very sorrowful: for he was very rich (Luke 18:18-23).

Now this man asked a good question. He knew that he would not live forever in this life and he wanted to have eternal life. And certainly Jesus is the right person to ask about eternal life. But you will notice that the ruler was "very sorrowful" over Jesus' response to his question.

What a fine person this rich ruler was. His character must have been beyond reproach. He was good morally, he honored his parents, he had from his youth up tried to do all that was right; but he knew that he lacked something. The character of this young ruler reminded me of Kim.

Kim and her boyfriend came to me for counseling prior to marriage. My convictions are strong. I am appalled by the high divorce rate, and I will only marry born-again Christians. I believe that a Christian wedding demands two Christians.

First, I asked the young man to tell me about his conversion. He related how he grew up in a Christian home and how he had received Christ as his Savior when he was just a young boy.

Then I asked Kim to tell me when she was born again.

"Well, I don't know what you mean by 'born again.' But I've been brought up in a Christian home, and I've gone to Sunday School and church, and I try to live a good life. I even went to a summer camp and I guess it was there that I was born again probably."

I showed Kim in the third chapter of John's Gospel the teachings of Jesus about the necessity of being born again (John 3:3, 3:5, and 3:7). And I explained that night to Kim how each of us needs to be saved. Since not one of us is perfect, we need a savior. The Bible declares that "all have sinned, and come short of the glory of God" (Romans 3:23). I commended her for being a morally good person and a religious person, but then I showed her that even in her life she could only get to Heaven through Jesus Christ. There is only one way to Heaven and that is through Jesus Christ. Together we read:

Thomas saith unto him, Lord, we know not whither thou goest; and how can we know the way? Jesus saith unto him, I am the way, the truth, and the life: no man cometh unto the Father, but by me (John 14:5-6).

"Kim, if you could go to Heaven by living a good life, then there would have been no necessity for Jesus' death on the cross."

Her eyes got large as she thought about it. Then she began to realize that Jesus died on that cross for her, that He bore her sins in His own body on the tree that He might pay her sin debt and bring her to God, so that she might become a child of God through faith.

I compared receiving Jesus as her Savior with taking her boy friend as her husband. Both require making a decision and following through upon the basis of that decision. For instance, she and her boy friend would enter the church as single people. But at the time in the service that they made their marriage vows, she would become his and he would become hers and they would have no right to any other. "Jesus wants to become yours and wants you for His own. He has already finished all that is necessary to enter into that relationship with you. But you must make a decision and act upon it to consummate that relationship. Before He can become your Savior, you must recognize that you are a sinner in need of a Savior and want with all your heart for Him to forgive your sins and come into your life to be your Savior and Lord."

That night in my study Kim bowed her knees to the Son of God and asked Christ to become her Savior and Lord. And what a testimony she became. She could relate to people who are good, but who are lost unless they have accepted as their Savior the gift of God, Jesus Christ.

The rich young ruler we read about could say to Jesus that he had kept the five commandments that Jesus mentioned on that occasion, but Jesus pointed out that he lacked one thing. In his case, he was depending too much upon all his wealth, and the truth of the matter is that we can depend upon nothing or no one but Jesus Christ for our salvation. Faith in Him. I believe the way to spell "faith" is F-A-I-T-H . . . forsaking all, I take Him.

The rich young ruler did the wrong thing, and he went away sorrowfully. Kim made the right decision. She went away rejoicing.

Have you made the right decision? If you have never invited Jesus Christ to come into your life to be your Lord and Savior, you can **do it right now and go on your way joyfully.**

Chapter 36

ESPECIALLY FOR YOU

As it is written, There is none righteous, no, not one: There is none that understandeth, there is none that seeketh after God (Romans 3:10-11).

If you are an unbeliever, or if you don't know for sure that you are a saved believer, and you have read all the chapters in this book, I believe that God is seeking you to give you an understanding of your need of the Savior and of the fact that the Savior died to meet your need.

For whosoever shall call upon the name of the Lord shall be saved (Romans 10:13).

"Whosoever shall call upon the name of the Lord shall be saved." That "whosoever" means you! You didn't understand, you didn't seek after God, but somehow this book got into your hands, and God the Holy Spirit has been speaking to you.

For whosoever shall call upon the name of the Lord shall be saved. How then shall they call on him in whom they have not believed? and how shall they believe in him of whom they have not heard? and how shall they hear without a preacher? And how shall they preach, except they be sent? (Romans 10:13-15)

I am certain that by reading this book you can believe. You can call upon the name of the Lord. And you can be saved!

These things have I written unto you that believe on the name of the Son of God; that ye may know that ye have eternal life, and that ye may believe on the name of the Son of God (1 John 5:13).

These things are written in the Bible that you might know, right now, that you have eternal life. The Bible is so important because it is the written Word of God that tells us about Jesus Christ, the living Word of God, who wants to give you eternal life.

The reason that you need God's gift of eternal life is that you are a sinner just like I am and everyone else is. God puts all of us in the same category:

For all have sinned, and come short of the glory of God (Romans 3:23).

You know you have sinned. I know that I have sinned. We don't know anyone who is perfect. God is a holy God. God is a righteous God. He is a just God. He cannot condone sin. In the Book of Ezekiel, we read: "the soul that sinneth, it shall die." Romans 6:23 says, "the wages of sin is death." Hebrews 9:27 states: "And as it is appointed unto men once to die, but after this the judgment." If you are not saved, you are not ready to die. But God is not willing that you should perish:

For God so loved the world, that he gave his only begotten Son, that whosoever believeth in him should not perish, but have everlasting life (John 3:16).

God so loved **you.** You can put your name there, dear "Whosoever". God loved you so much that He gave His only Son to pay your sin debt so that you can be reconciled to a holy God and have everlasting life. Why did God give His Son? It is the only way you can be saved. God can't be a just God and take sinners to Heaven apart from Jesus Christ. If the wages of sin is death, someone had to die. God's love provided that Someone. The baby that was born in Bethlehem's manger was the Son that was given. He grew into manhood and never knew any sin. Jesus made His way to the cross of Calvary where He willingly laid down His life to redeem us from our sins. He was buried but He arose the third day, according to the Scriptures. He has provided salvation for you and for me. **But we have to appropriate, or claim, that salvation which he has provided.** By a simple, child-like faith each of us must call upon the name of the Lord in repentance for our sins and ask Him to come into our lives to be our Savior.

What does it mean to "call upon the name of the Lord"? It means that you believe the Word of God. You believe, or realize, that you are a sinner. You believe that when Jesus died upon the cross of Calvary for the sins of the world **that He died for your sins.** You believe that He is alive today, and you call upon Him and ask Him to come into your life as your personal Savior. He will save you!

But as many as received him, to them gave he power to become the sons of God, even to them that believe on his name (John 1:12).

Behold, what manner of love the Father hath bestowed upon us, that we should be called the sons of God (1 John 3:1).

Wouldn't you like to thank God right now for His great love, for your opportunity to hear and read the Gospel, for meeting your every need, and for saving you right now, right where you are, if you ask Him to and receive Him through faith? He tells us plainly that "whosoever shall call upon the name of the Lord shall be saved."

My purpose in writing this book, and I'm sure God's purpose in having you read this book, is that you might know Him as your Lord and Savior.

We would appreciate it very much if you would write and tell us how you received a copy of this book, how God spoke to your heart through it, and how God finished the work by showing you your personal need of Christ as your Lord and Savior.

We would cherish that information. You would become another chapter. Oh, not in this book, of course, but your name will have been written in the Lamb's Book of Life.

Dear friend, for a word of assurance, I want to close this book with these words:

And this is the record, that God hath given to us eternal life, and this life is in his Son. He that hath the Son hath life; and he that hath not the Son of God hath not life (1 John 5:11-12).

It's up to you, dear friend. What will you do with Jesus?

C. Jack Orr A 216
211 Willow Valley Square
Lancaster, PA 17602

143